SECRETS of BUYING THE RIGHT BUSINESS *(for you)* RIGHT

A ROADMAP TO YOUR FAMILY BUSINESS

Ed Pendarvis, CBI (Fellow of IBBA)
Business Broker, STUDENT/TEACHER
Sunbelt Founder, Chairman Emeritus

Copyright © 2009 by Edward T. Pendarvis. All rights reserved. Printed in the United States of America. Except as permitted under the United States Copyright Act of 1976, no part of this publication may be reproduced or distributed in any form or by any means, or stored in a database or retrieval system, without the prior written permission of the publisher.

ISBN: 1-4392-6435-X
ISBN-13: 9781439264355

This publication is designed to provide accurate and authoritative information in regard to the subject matter covered. It is sold with the understanding that neither the author nor the publisher is engaged in rendering legal, accounting, futures/securities trading, or other professional service. If legal advice or other expert assistance is required, the services of a competent professional person should be sought.

> — *From a declaration of principles jointly adopted by a Committee of the American Bar Association and a Committee of Publishers.*

This book and video are dedicated to . . .

America's family business owners in our hometowns - both present and future. They make "Main Street" work even when "Wall Street" doesn't. They are our neighbors.

They get up every day, usually before sunrise, to open their businesses to provide goods and services that make our lives better, provide jobs for others and contribute greatly to the quality of our lives and our communities and our country.

They are "America's Amazing Economic Engine" that celebrates and nurtures the entrepreneurial spirit that has made this the greatest economy in history. They are part of the American Dream of business owners - they create value.

GOOD for THEM, GOOD for US!

Ed Pendarvis, Sunbelt Founder, and Sunbelt Office owners welcome Peter Shea, CEO of Entrepreneur Media, Inc. as keynote speaker to the Sunbelt Annual Meeting in San Diego, California in 2004.

Members of the Class of 1965 attend the Business School Hall of Fame Dinner at the Citadel's Holliday Alumni Center. Edward T. Pendarvis (holding award, center) was one of the 2007 Honorees.

Contents

	Preface	ix
Chapter 1	Decisions	1
Chapter 2	Start Up/Buy Existing /Buy A Franchise?	11
Chapter 3	What Are You Buying? – Earnings (Lifestyle)	17
Chapter 4	Business Size Makes a Difference	23
Chapter 5	Value Drivers of a Business	31
Chapter 6	How Do You Find the Right Business?	37
Chapter 7	Focus Is Important	41
Supplement	The Family Business, the Family Farm	47

Chapter 8	How Much Can I Make?	53
Chapter 9	Financing, the "Mother's Milk" of Buying and Selling	61
Chapter 10	Negotiate with a Buyer/Seller-Friendly Offer	71
Chapter 11	Due Diligence – (Never Fun and Easy)	85
Chapter 12	Closing the Purchase and Taking over Ownership	95
Appendix	Sample Forms and Agreements	113
	About the Author	131

Preface

WOW! 2008 was an interesting year. The "Earthquake on Wall Street" has redefined our national economy and helped recalibrate our personal economic world at about 65 percent of where most folks were. Our home value and home equity may be down, our personal retirement portfolio is down, and our job security is down. If you still had a job after the meltdown of the housing market, the financial markets, the stock markets, the auto industry, $4 per gallon gas prices, and a low consumer confidence level that has translated into a very slow retail recovery . . . you were doing pretty well. But, for how long?

Did you see the longtime employees of Lehman Brothers walking out of their headquarters building on Wall Street in New York last year with their "jobs and other possessions" in cardboard boxes? As the unemployment numbers rise, are YOU ready for, or do you dread the possibility that, a "pink slip" might be in your future - perhaps through absolutely "NO FAULT" of your own? I maintain that the prospects for economic stability and growth are far better on Main Street

PREFACE

than they are on Wall Street. And this may be the best time for you to consider going into business for yourself and providing for your own job security.

That is exactly why I wrote this book. You have some very good and powerful options available to you in the "world of work" that I believe you should consider. And these opportunities are available to you right in your hometown where you live or want to live. One of those options is to OWN YOUR OWN BUSINESS - "You Can Do It," as Home Depot says, and, "I can help."

Just as I have helped thousands of other buyers and sellers of businesses over the last thirty years, and just as I have helped train thousands of business brokers as I helped build Sunbelt (www.sunbeltnetwork.com - click on tab "About Us" for more information) into the largest business brokerage network in the world with hundreds of offices and thousands of brokers in the United States and thirty foreign countries.

However, I do not believe that this goal can successfully be reached simply by purchasing and reading a book - this one or any other one. It will take some specific decisions, actions, and "heavy lifting" on your part in concert with expert, experienced, and professional advice and counsel. We have laid out a road map to help you follow a proven step-by-step process (protected all the way as best as is possible), to finding, valuing, negotiating, financing, buying, and owning your own successful business.

Although the process may have some cost and risk (some known and some unknown at this point), the potential results are priceless! (And, any cost and risk will be defined, disclosed and discussed ahead of time - I do not like surprises, unless they are happy surprises, and I'll bet you don't either.)

This process or journey will be a "partnership" between you and me. We will develop a **TEAM APPROACH** to assist you in reaching your goal. Our **TEAM** will consist of you, the buyer, me, the buyer's agent and advisor, the seller (who wants or needs to sell), any local business broker involved, accountants and lawyers as needed, landlords, lenders, and anyone else that would like to see a successful transaction between you and a seller.

We will incorporate many of the steps listed below and others, as the need arises. We will be:

1. Sharing experiences, processes and procedures, and recommendations as laid out in the chapters and pages of this book

2. Sharing ideas, back ground, methods and "war stories" based on years of successful business deals in DVD and CD formats, to enhance your and your spouse's comfort level and understanding of the book information

3. Offering live telephone, Webinar, e-mail, and SKYPE conferences (in groups/one-on-one)

PREFACE

4. Offering actual business buyer's agency and advisor services to quarterback the team to assist YOU in locating and buying the right business (for you) - right

5. Using industry databases, experience, and valuation methodology to help arrive at fair and workable prices, terms and conditions on the business

You want to buy a business and the seller wants and/or needs to sell a business. This should not be an adversarial process. You are both trying to get to your own goal line. The good news is, . . . it is the exact same goal line. A business deal that allows you to buy a business that will provide a living for you and your family and, at the same time, allows the seller to exit the business and get paid for the value of the business. You both win!

Forget Wall Street. (Wall Street has most certainly already forgotten you.) Make the decision now, this day, to invest in a sure thing - INVEST IN YOURSELF. Decide to be a part of the American Dream and own your own business. Go to work each day and for the rest of your life on behalf of the man or woman you look at in the mirror. He or she always has you and your family's best interest at heart and they won't fire you in midcareer.

You just may accomplish three very important things:

> ONE – You have a job for life (you are probably not going to fire yourself);

TWO – You have the opportunity to make more $$$$ (most every big business started off as a small business);

THREE – You are building equity in something that you own and can sell later, if you wish (you cannot sell your job).

Today truly is the first day of the rest of your life. If not now - WHEN? If not you - WHO? If not where you live - WHERE? Life is not a dress rehearsal. Your future and my future is here and now. And, I would consider it a personal honor and privilege to assist you in making the right decision for you and your family in "Buying the Right Business (for you) Right."

Simply order or download a copy of my book and the DVD segments on the process, and let's get started. You can e-mail me or call me for a FREE confidential initial consultation.

E-mail me at:
edpendarvis@businessbuyersuniversity.com
or call me at
(843) 789-4112

Best Wishes and Respect,
Ed Pendarvis, CBI (Fellow of IBBA)
Business Broker, STUDENT/TEACHER
Sunbelt Founder, Chairman Emeritus

1
DECISIONS

CONGRATULATIONS! You are the person that has the responsibility of being the breadwinner in your family and you have made the decision to look at all of the possibilities of making a good living for yourself and your family, including owning your own business. **GOOD FOR YOU!**

In most cases that journey started long ago with a "paying job." You may have started earning your own money with an after-school, weekend, or summer job. However, once you became a grown-up, the part-time job was replaced by a real, full-time job that provided an income for you.

If you were determined enough and fortunate enough to graduate from high school, tech school, college, had military experience and training, or a postgraduate degree, your chances of getting a better-paying job were greatly enhanced. Through the development and use of your skills and talents, both learned and "God given," you have added value to your employer and hopefully, grown with your employer - both in job status and income.

1: DECISIONS

While that has worked for you so far, you have probably also noticed that there is a limit to your opportunities as an employee - both in growth potential and income potential. And, as you "play down the board," there is very little chance that you will (1) stay in that job for life (either by your choice or by circumstances that you do not control) or (2) ever become wealthy working for someone else.

Please think about this: what do you need from a job? You need an income. You need an income to provide a "lifestyle" for yourself and your family. You need an income to make the house payments, the car payments, and to feed and educate your children. You need an income to provide for trips, vacations, new and bigger "stuff," and for "the pursuit of happiness" (however you may define it). And, you need an income to provide for eventual retirement.

There are basically two ways for you to provide an income for you and your family - you can work for someone else or you can work for yourself. Both have rewards and both have risks. And, as Brian Tracy, noted business coach and author of several excellent business books says, "either way, when you think about it, you are always working for yourself." The difference is that in the first case you are helping to build someone else's business, and in the second case you are building your own business.

I believe, with all my heart, that you are far, far better off using your skills and talents to build your own business. And, incidentally, there are reasons that owning your own business is often referred to as the American Dream. We will explore several of these reasons in this book, on DVDs and in Webinars, as well as show you how you may apply them to your own and your family's benefit.

Now, that does not mean that it is easy, or that "dreaming" will get you there; however, everything begins with a dream, an idea. That is followed by desire and decisions, followed by planning, preparation, and specific actions that move you in the direction of your dreams.

You have taken a very important first step by picking up this book. DO NOT STOP!

I can help you and I can work with you and show you how to marshal several other good, experienced professionals in your community to help you. I have spent my work life helping folks just like you to value, sell, and/or buy existing successful businesses and franchises. Hopefully, you will look at your options and decide to look further into the process of "How To Buy the Right Business (for you) Right."

This is a very specific process, and, while it is not necessarily easy, it is definable, and it definitely is important. In fact, it just may be the second-most important decision that you will ever make in your adult life. (How are you going to provide an income or lifestyle for yourself and your family?)

The most important decision that you will probably ever make in your adult life is choosing a spouse. It has been said that 90 percent of your future happiness and success (or lack thereof) may be tied to that one decision. Since I do not claim any qualifications in affairs of the heart, I would not touch that decision with a ten-foot pole. However, the second-most important decision is how you are going to provide a living for yourself and your family through buying a business, which is my specialty - it is what I do.

With the Lord's help, and with the help of very good friends and associates, I founded and built Sunbelt into the largest business brokerage franchise network in the world. I have personally sold or helped manage the sale of over one thousand businesses, in all categories, over the last thirty years. Now Sunbelt sells one thousand businesses every three to four months. COOL!

I have also learned a great deal from other professionals in business brokerages over the last twenty years as an active member/student/teacher/participant and board member in our industry trade group, the International Business Brokers Association (IBBA), www.ibba.org. As I have traveled around the United States, Canada, and the United Kingdom I have been surprised and pleased at how small, private businesses sales and transactions work, with some degree of similarity, in all fifty states and all around the world.

I have also been pleased and impressed with the education, experience, market knowledge, ethics, and value that a good business broker brings to the marketplace - for both the seller and the buyer. That can be important to you as we move through this process because of the confidentiality of business sales - it is very difficult to find a good business that is for sale in your community. There are no "for sale" signs like you see in real estate sales.

Each deal has a very important seller that is probably selling his or her largest and most valuable asset, except for the seller's family, of course, and the seller probably wants as much as he or she can get for the business. Each deal also has a very important buyer that is risking a substantial portion of his or her life savings in buying a business to obtain the owner's benefit that the business provides, and the buyer wants to pay as little as possible and does not like risk.

Somewhere in there is a fair deal, with price, terms, and conditions that work for both sides. And, keep in mind . . .we are usually not dealing with a foolish seller nor are we dealing with a foolish buyer. (Nor do we want to be.) For the deal to work, it has to work for everyone involved. The seller is probably going to have to take a little less than he or she wants to and the buyer is probably going to have to pay a little more than he or she wants to.

Also, for the deal to make sense, the owner's benefit has to be enough for the buyer to make a living and pay the debt service on the purchase as well as the other business expenses - or No Deal.

There is always a way to get there. However, before we approach the step-by-step process of making decisions on buying a business, let's look first at the process of decision making itself. Most all decisions, big and small, include these two steps:

1. It is a subconscious or conscious process of elimination that leads to a decision, and

1: DECISIONS

2. It is encased in an all-things-considered decision that leads to action.

Let's start with the first, a subconscious or conscious process of elimination. When you bought your house that you live in now, didn't you look at several houses - perhaps different styles, different neighborhoods, different school districts? And for whatever reasons, you decided on the house that you did. When you bought your car, didn't you look at several different types and models of cars - different colors, different features, different dealerships? When you and your spouse got married, had you not dated others first?

For whatever reason or reasons - you eliminated the other choices and you chose this house, this car, this person. And, when you go out to eat - fast food or sit-down dining - they present you with a menu with from ten to thirty items that you could choose, and you choose "___." All of these are a conscious, or a subconscious process of elimination. We choose the things that we want or like and we eliminate the things that we don't want or like. The results are the same - a decision, given the options that we have, about what we like.

Sometimes the second, all things considered, is a little more difficult to pinpoint. For instance, in making a decision to buy a house. All things considered, do we absolutely have and need to buy that house? Would the present house or apartment not do for a while longer? Do we have to have that car, or can we continue with our present arrangement? Do we have to get married, or could we not just continue to date for a while longer? We do have options; however, at some point, all things considered (given the options that we have available), we decide on and choose "____."

Well, that same process is the logical one that we will follow in this book, DVDs, CDs, Webinars, teleconferences, and business buyer agent and advisory conferences that make up a "holistic" approach that I believe is necessary to help you in making the best and right decision for you and your family. It is important to you and to me.

So, to really help you and add value to your process, I believe that I have to work with you just as I would if you e-mailed me, called me, or came into my Sunbelt office in Charleston, Myrtle Beach, Hilton Head, South Carolina, or Savannah, Georgia. We need to work as a TEAM; and to be successful as a TEAM, we have to define our relationship so that we know what we can expect from each other and how to proceed.

I believe that:

1. I have to get to know you.

2. You have got to get to know me.

3. We have to get local, trusted, professional help.

4. We have to have a menu of services to select from.

1: DECISIONS

5. We have to understand each other's roles and responsibilities, and hopefully.

6. We have to like and trust each other.

This is a major decision that can have a huge and important impact on your family. And, just as in the medical profession, where there is a process, sequence, and procedure that the doctor follows: "examination, diagnosis, and then prescription" (and, prescription without examination and diagnosis is malpractice), there is a process, sequence, and procedure that we will follow. Your health is far too important to be handled without examination and diagnosis. Well, I maintain that your economic health is also far too important to be handled without examination and diagnosis. So we will utilize both, as a TEAM, and do our very best to write the right prescription for you.

Please note that I am not a lawyer or an accountant, and I am not qualified to give legal or accounting advice. Furthermore, even though I am and have been a real estate broker in South Carolina for over thirty years; I will not give you real estate advice or charge any fees pertaining to real estate. There will be times in the process when I will recommend that you seek legal and accounting advice. And keep in mind that all of the information on a specific business will be provided by the seller. The seller is the source of and responsible for all of the financial and other information that he or she provides about his or her business.

This is exciting - This is important and, no matter what, I congratulate you. You have taken the first very important step in owing a part of the American Dream of owning your own business for you and your family. It is my greatest hope that this book, its information, and this relationship will provide an easy-to-follow road map and prove to be of great value to you in making the right decisions and in getting you to your goal line.

Let's **GET STARTED!**

2
START UP/BUY EXISTING/BUY A FRANCHISE?

OK - Let's say that the first decision has been made. Now, or soon, you want to grab for the brass ring and go into business for yourself to make a living. You are choosing a path followed by Henry Ford, George Eastman, John Deere, Ray Kroc, Colonel Harland Sanders, Dave Thomas, Sam Walton, Ted Turner, Michael Dell, Oprah Winfrey, Bill Gates, and Martha Stewart. They all began with a small business, something that they liked and believed in, and with a lot of hard work, some course corrections, more hard work (and perhaps some divine intervention and a little luck), they built big and successful businesses.

These folks, and most other successful business people have three very important things in common:

1. They made decisions quickly and easily.

2. They liked what they were doing.

3. They owned their own businesses.

While all three things are important, I believe that 2 - they liked what they were doing - is probably the most important. You should keep these three things in mind as we move through the process. It is very important to find a business that you like. You will probably be spending more "awake time" in your business than you will be with your family (24 hours in a day, less 8 hours sleep, less 8–10 hours at work, less 1–2 hours travel = 4–7 hours left). That's all right, you are the breadwinner, you are working for your family; however, you will be a lot better "family man or woman" if you like your work. And, you are human - you will always be more successful if you enjoy what you are doing.

As you make decisions, making decisions becomes easier. You set out on a course or a direction and start down that path and when you do there is a principle that will help you called the "corridor principle." Think of a corridor in a building. You may not be able to see too far down the corridor just standing there. As you move down the corridor, however, you become aware of doors, windows, closets, stairs, skylights, bulletin boards, entrances, elevators, exits, and additional hallways that you never would have seen if you had not started down that corridor.

In order to make the best decisions for you as we move through this process, we need to start by gathering as many facts and figures as we need; search for as much good information as is available and consider as many options and possibilities as are necessary. Study them and then select the best options for you. And, as we move down this corridor, additional options may appear.

There will be a series of small, medium, and large decisions that you will have to make as we proceed. It is also very important that we make sure that you are protected all along the way in this process. I will attempt to do that by keeping you informed, preparing you for the next step, and suggesting that we take one step at a time.

Now, I like analogies, so let's say that there are several bridges that we have to cross to get you to your goal. All of these bridges have to be crossed and they are all important and necessary, and they need to be considered. However, let's not let that overwhelm us. Whereas, some folks say, "We need to make sure that we agree on all of these ten–eleven bridges before we cross the first bridge," I respectfully disagree. Let's cross one bridge at a time. If we do not get across the first bridge, the remaining ten bridges do not matter.

Another analogy in finding and buying the right business is that it is kind of like finding the right mate and getting married. You would not go to the church dance, see someone you think is good looking, walk over and say, "Would you like to dance, get married, have four children and live in double-wide in Missoula, Montana?" would you? Let's just start off with, "Would you like to dance?" If that doesn't work - nothing else matters. In finding and buying the right business - let's start

2: START UP/BUY EXISTING/BUY A FRANCHISE?

with the first decision, get by that and then take the next step, then the next, etc.

The real payoff to you and your family is in owning and growing your family business. You can add great value to your family's wealth by growing the value of your business. By far and away, the best route to personal and business wealth in America is through owning your own business. Day trading and flipping houses pale in comparison to the wealth that can be built in a successful family business.

So let's say that your first big decision has been made - you want to own your own business. The second big decision is (1) Do you want to start up a business, (2) Do you want to buy an existing business, or (3) Do you want to buy a franchise business? Each has some advantages and some disadvantages. Let's look at them individually.

First, a start-up. Whereas, this may seem the least expensive initially, US Department of Commerce statistics show that 65–90 percent of start-up businesses are not still in business after five years. There are many reasons for those numbers. One of the main ones being that no matter what type of business you start up, you have to get people (customers) to stop going wherever they have been going to get that product and/or service, and come and buy that product and/or service from you. And, you normally start with the normal costs and expenses (rent, inventory, furniture, fixtures, equipment, leasehold improvements, employees, training, advertising, insurance, etc.), and at first you have no customers and no sales (no income).

How long will you have to "burn" through your start-up cash before you start "cash flowing"? That means taking in more income through sales of your products and/or services than it cost you in cost of goods sold and expenses to produce those sales and operate the business. Can you and your family go for "XXXX" weeks/months/years without an income? Remember, in owning your own business, you are paid only "after" all of the other expenses have been paid.

Obviously, start-ups sometimes work very well, especially, if you have a product and/or service that is new and different and the marketplace accepts your new business. In most cases, however, I do not recommend starting up a business.

Second, buying an existing business. The same statistics that apply to the failure rate of small businesses show that if you buy an existing successful business (it already has trained employees, an existing customer base - existing sales, and an established cash flow - sufficient to pay the business' expenses and provide the owner with a living), there is a 90–95 percent chance that the business will still be in business after five years (provided, of course, that you buy it right).

Third, buying a successful franchise. The 90 percent plus success rate applies to buying a successful franchise also, provided that the franchise has already proven the market's acceptance of that franchise concept. This may be true even though the franchise that you buy may be a start-up in that location. For example, you are starting up a donut shop, and the franchise company has twenty-eight hundred other stores that have proved

2: START UP/BUY EXISTING/BUY A FRANCHISE?

successful in making and selling donuts. There is a pretty good chance that your franchise start-up will be successful.

Each of these business opportunities have some advantages and some disadvantages that we will discuss in the following chapters. As we look at your options, keep in mind that business brokers sell business opportunities, they do not sell business guarantees. In fact, if someone were to guarantee you success in a business venture, I would be very skeptical of that person and that business venture.

In business, in marriage, in life - we make the BEST DECISION, the BEST GUESS, that we can based on the best data, education, experience, and information available - then we add to the mixture two things: (1) that all important dose of common sense that the good Lord has given to all of us, and (2) a gut feeling that usually helps us make the right decision - or at least helps prevent us from making the wrong decision.

I am a big proponent of buying an existing successful business and working hard to first maintain that success and then to grow the business through the improvements that you make to management and to the business. It is the same rationale that big businesses use in merger and acquisition (M and A). They merge and acquire another business that has a product and/or service that has proven itself in the marketplace rather than starting a business from scratch. Most every big business has grown through buying another existing business that already had market share, customers, trained employees, cash flow, etc.

Now comes – ALL THINGS CONSIDERED!

3
WHAT ARE YOU BUYING? – EARNINGS (LIFESTYLE)

OK – Let's say that the second decision has been made. All things considered, you and your family see that the safest and best option for you to get to your goal of making a living (by owning your own business), is to buy an existing successful business or a successful franchise in a community where you live or wish to live. Uniquely, either way, you will have the opportunity of being in business for yourself, but not by yourself.

The existing business owner, who knows more about that business than anyone else in the world, or the franchisor, who knows more about that franchise than anyone else in the world, will have a vested financial interest in your success and they will help you to learn how to manage and operate the business successfully. That is a good way to start.

Please understand, no matter what kind of job you have, whether you are a clerk, a construction worker, a nurse, a school

3: WHAT ARE YOU BUYING? – EARNINGS (LIFESTYLE)

teacher, a counter salesperson, a stock broker, a delivery person, a computer programmer, an outside salesperson, a server, a vice president of "XX," what you need out of that job is an income. No matter what kind of business you buy, a retail business, a service business, a manufacturing business, a distribution business, a restaurant, a bar/lounge, a convenience store, a dry cleaners, an auto repair shop, a liquor store - what you need out of that business is an income. And you need an income as quickly as possible.

Therein lies one of the most important advantages of buying an existing business. An immediate income! An existing successful business should provide enough income to pay the business' expenses, pay the debt service on the acquisition, and give you and your family an immediate income. It is already "up and running" and has been paying the business' expenses and providing the present owner, the seller and his or her family, an income for several years.

Now, since you are the breadwinner in your family and since any decision that you make concerning your job or your business affects both you and your family - in the interest of brevity, going forward, I will use "you" to mean both you and your family. That will help me not get tired of having to spell that out each time and, hopefully, help you not get too tired of reading it each time.

So, let's look at exactly what are you buying when you buy an existing business. Normally, you will be buying the assets of the business: the furniture, fixtures, equipment, inventory, leasehold improvements, trademarks, trade names, trade secrets, tangible and intangible assets, brand names, patients, customer list, and all other assets of the business (except cash and accounts receivable). You will normally not be buying any existing liabilities of the business and you will not normally be buying the corporate shares of stock (if the seller is a corporation).

You are buying an existing, ongoing economic entity that is providing a product and/or service (or a combination of both) that customers and clients respond to by buying that business' product and/or service in sufficient quantities to provide the business' owner with enough income to pay all operating costs and expenses and, hopefully, also provide an income (or lifestyle) for the owner. That income is sometimes referred to as income, earnings, cash flow, owner's benefit, seller's discretionary earnings (SDE), or seller's discretionary cash flow (SDCF). It is also sometimes referred to incorrectly as profit.

For our purposes, let's use the definition that IBBA uses for SDE or SDCF. These owner's benefit SDE - "Adjusted earnings before taxes, interest income or expenses, non-operating and non-recurring income/expenses, depreciation, amortization, and other non-cash charges and prior to deducting an owner's/officer's compensation." To make it simpler, let's use another of my analogies.

Let's say that the income (sales) and expenses are like water backing up behind a dam. The top of the dam represents the break-even point. Everything below the top of the dam represents non-discretionary expenses or operating costs of the business that are necessary to produce that income (sales). They would be costs of goods sold, rent, advertising, employee cost, insurance, electric, phones, etc. Until and unless the income and sales get above the top of the dam - there is no income or discretionary cash flow for the owner. However, any and all income and cash flow "above the top of the dam" is the seller's discretionary earnings or cash flow. That is the true owner's benefit.

The owner can use any and all of that money any way he or she wishes. The owner can use that cash flow to buy more inventory, to advertise more, to pay off debts, to take a trip, buy a house, car, or boat, or pay him or herself more money, or whatever - it is owner's benefit. And if the owner is selling the business, it is the SDE that helps define value.

THAT IS A VERY IMPORTANT NUMBER!

From a valuation point of view, it is very important because most businesses are valued and sold based on some acceptable multiple of SDE. From your standpoint, it is very important because if you buy the business, and you run the business in a similar fashion that the seller did (and you did a similar amount of sales and maintained similar expenses), you should expect to have a similar SDE, less whatever new debt service (expenses) you would have. We will be talking a lot about that later.

When I am training business brokers for Sunbelt, or when I am teaching an IBBA course in recasting, pricing, or negotiating, the subject of business value almost always comes up. While I will devote another chapter to specifically answering that important question, it always leads me to ask my students two basic questions to set a foundation for determining value.

First, what is the purpose of a business? Many answers come up such as, "The purpose of a business is to provide a product and/or service that the marketplace responds favorably to." "The purpose of a business is to catch and keep customers." "The purpose of a business is to serve your marketplace." OK, all of those things have some application; however, I believe that the basic purpose of a business is to MAKE A LIVING FOR THE OWNER.

Second, I like to ask my fellow students what they would consider to be a good business. As we go around the room, many folks express what type of business they would consider a good business. Some say retail, some service, some manufacturing, distribution, tech related, food service, etc. And, many of them express an opinion of what they do not think is a good business. We all have preferences and prejudices, do we not? OK, again, all of those things have some application; and they are true and honest opinions.

Let me ask you these questions. Have you not seen good businesses in each of those categories in your town or city (retail, service, manufacturing, restaurants, etc.)? However, I believe that if the first item - that the basic purpose of a business is to make a living for the owner is true (and I submit to you that it is), then I would also submit to you that every business, on every side of the road, and every side road, that has been in operation for three years or longer fits the base definition of a good business. It is obviously making someone a living or it would not still be in business. The question for you is - would it be a good business for you?

Now, we still need to get a lot of information to even begin to arrive at value of a specific business; however, one question can be answered pretty quickly. Do you like the business? Could you see yourself working in and working on this business for eight, ten, twelve hours per day; six or seven days per week? Would you be proud to say that you owned this business? Do you see the potential of your buying and growing this business?

Once those questions are answered, at least preliminarily, we will begin to look at the SDE, or cash flow, to see if that works for you. One thing that we know is that you are going to have to have a sufficient SDE to provide for your family's needs - the good news is that the seller's family has house payments, car payments, and kids that want to eat three times a day and that have to be educated just like yours.

One other opportunity is to find a business that is being run (managed) absentee. For instance, the owner is not the on-site manager. That may allow you to take over active on-site management and you would start by picking up the manger's salary and perks plus the present owner's benefit.

We will look at several different good businesses and using the "process of elimination," let's find one that may work for you. Additionally, I will give you several rules of thumb, or "Ed's Rules of Buyers" that we can use as sanity checks as we walk through this process of helping you find and Buy the Right Business (for you) Right.

4
BUSINESS SIZE MAKES A DIFFERENCE

The size of the business that you are looking at can make a difference in several ways. Some obvious, some not. We will divide businesses for our purposes into several different categories, by size, to help explain how these size differences may affect your search for your right business.

The largest businesses are normally publicly traded companies or corporations; their corporate shares of stock are traded (sold and bought) on the various stock exchanges. We are usually very familiar with these companies and oftentimes their names are household words - General Motors, Wal-Mart, General Electric, Coca Cola, IBM, Intel, Microsoft, Google, McDonald's, etc. These large businesses normally operate under a certain set of rules applicable to them. Let's call these "big business rules."

Smaller businesses that we will be dealing with may be corporations (C Corp., S Corp., LLC), partnerships of some definition, or sole proprietorships, in legal structure; regardless, they are not public companies. They are what are called

4: BUSINESS SIZE MAKES A DIFFERENCE

private companies. And while some of these private companies may still be large, they operate under an entirely different set of rules. Let's call these small-business rules.

Still another area of business differentiation, as far as rules are concerned, is based on the amount of the business' annual gross sales. Oftentimes the amount of, or volume of, annual gross sales may determine both the management style and record-keeping accuracy of the business. Since we normally think in terms of one year as annual income, the annual gross sales, hereinafter gross sales, can play a significant role in determining the earning capability, and therefore, the value of the business.

I have found that another dividing line in small business rules that affects management, financial record keeping, and earnings, comes when a business reaches a gross sales level of around $1 million in gross sales per year. In using $1million as the break point for our purposes, let's say that businesses that do $1million in gross sales, or less, operate under still another set of rules. Let's call these small-small-businesses rules.

Now, I like analogies, so going forward, since we will be dealing with different business rules for different size businesses, let's refer to these as follows:

1. big business rules - football rules

2. small business rules - basketball rules

3. real estate rules - soccer rules

4. small-small-business rules - baseball rules

While these are most certainly all ball games, they are also most certainly played by a different set of rules for each game. You cannot use football rules in a baseball game; you cannot play basketball on a football field - it simply will not work. And, you cannot use big business rules when trying to value and buy a small-small business - it simply will not work. So - let's look at how these rules differ.

Football rules apply in a business ball game played in businesses that may very well do millions or even billions of dollars in gross sales, or more. They are owned by shareholders (stockholders) and have a formal board of directors that represent the shareholders and that hire management to manage and run the day-to-day operation of the business. These management positions can consist of a chief executive officer (CEO), president, chief operating officer (COO), chief financial officer (CFO), and others. They have to have audited financial statements and they have to report basic financial statements to the public on a quarterly and annual basis. The audit has to be done by a qualified certified public accountant or accounting firm that certifies and professionally warrants the accuracy and completeness of the audited financials.

Footnote: Enron, WorldCom, Lehman Brothers, Citi, AIG, Chrysler, Wachovia, Washington Mutual, and GM all had audited financial statements.

4: BUSINESS SIZE MAKES A DIFFERENCE

Basketball rules apply to any privately owned business that does more than $1million in gross sales and, for our purposes, let's say up to $30 million in gross sales. Above that level of gross sales, a private company pretty much plays by football rules except for the public reporting. They usually have hired management in addition to the owner and they normally deal with audited financial statements. Below $30 million in sales, and especially below $5 million in gross sales, they may or may not deal with audited statements - most likely, they will have reviewed statements and the owner may also be the manager. However, the owner probably has a bookkeeper or bookkeeping section in addition to him or herself and, as in football rules, the owner uses the financial records to help manage the business.

Soccer rules - real estate, is one of the most "open" businesses in the world. There are thousands of real estate agents and brokers, big FOR SALE signs are placed on property to announce to the world that this property is for sale, mortgage bankers will normally lend up to 90 percent of value of an owner-occupied house based on comparable sales, and almost all real estate brokers co-broker sales. And all real estate transactions are recorded, including the selling price. Very public!

Baseball rules apply to any privately owned business that does less than $1 million in gross sales. The owner is usually also the day-to-day manager, the head salesperson, the PR person, the stock person, the bookkeeper, the janitor, and the person in charge of the checkbook. The owner hires, trains, manages, and fires employees. He or she is responsible only to him or herself and almost never has an audited or even a reviewed financial statement - the owner deals with a compiled statement in filing taxes. And all of the financial information that was turned into his accountant has been compiled by the owner. He or she knows more about this business than anyone else in the world.

Interestingly enough, 95 percent of the twenty-four million private businesses in the United States of America fall in the range of baseball rules; another 3 percent fall in the range of basketball rules. That is, of course, counting a company like Coca Cola as one company and counting your neighborhood convenience store as one business. Isn't it strange that 98 percent of are all businesses are small businesses; yet everything that you study in school and college about business involves big business rules, everything on business TV shows involves talking heads of big business, and everything that you read in the business section of the newspaper is about big business. The good news is that most of the real opportunities are in small-small business and now you will be armed with the knowledge and information necessary for you to understand the rules that apply to these businesses - baseball rules.

Here following is my first "Ed's Rules of Buyers," based on my experience in selling or helping my fellow business brokers to sell thousands of businesses over the last thirty years. Keep in mind a very important premise that SALES DRIVES VALUE. That bears repeating. SALES DRIVES VALUE. If there are no sales or low sales, that business entity has no value or low value. Sales are the market's response to that business' product and/or service. Therefore gross sales helps define the value of

4: BUSINESS SIZE MAKES A DIFFERENCE

the business because the real bottom line of earnings (SDE) has to come out of the top line of gross sales.

A pretty good rule of thumb for determining potential earnings, SDE, on a business that has been in business for at least three years or longer, and is doing $1 million or less in gross sales, is that an owner/manager could make from 10 percent to 20 percent of gross sales, SDE. For instance, if the business is doing $622,000 in gross sales, the owner/manager could make from $60,000 to around $120,000 per year, depending on how the business is run. A business doing around $400,000 in gross sales could potentially make the owner/manager $40,000 to $80,000, depending on the management. Of course, the business may not be making that much SDE. However, that is a range of possible earnings. And, if we are interested, at the appropriate time, we will ask the owner to "show us the money" to help us determine how much owner's benefit or SDE is available.

Once a business gets above the $1 million mark in gross sales level, the potential earnings, owner's benefit (SDE) for the owner/manager, goes down quickly to around 10 percent or less of gross sales. For instance, if the business is doing $5,200,000 in gross sales, the owner/manager may be making from $250,000 to $400,000. That's a lot of money, however, under 10 percent of gross sales. The reason is that normally the larger business has more management cost, more inventory, and perhaps thinner margins.

How do we really know how much a business is making? We ask the only person who truly knows - the owner, the seller.

And, we want the truth, the whole truth, and nothing but the truth. And all the way through this process, we have found it to be a very good policy to use former President Ronald Reagan's wise adage, "Trust, but verify!" However, as a start, I think that you will find the rule of thumb of 10–20 percent of gross sales will put you in a ballpark of potential earnings and serve as a "sanity check" for determining earnings. And it will go a long way in answering a most important question.

"If I buy this business, how much could I make a year?" The best answer for the question, "How much can I make?" begins with the answer, "How much is the present owner making now?" We'll see.

5
VALUE DRIVERS OF A BUSINESS

What is the value of the business and what is the value of the business to you? Both of those things are very important and they both have to be answered. They may not be the same answer, as well as the fact that there are many different approaches to the answers. Since we are primarily looking at how buying a business will provide you an income sufficient to provide an acceptable lifestyle, we will normally focus on the past, present, and future earnings of the business. The best and most reliable projections of future earnings are based on the most recent past and the present.

For example, what was happening in the real estate market, the stock market, or the automobile market two years ago has almost nothing to do with what is happening in those markets today or with what may happen in the near future. And while the financial records of the business that we are interested in are important for determining value and future earnings, the information that they give us is only as accurate as the information itself.

5: VALUE DRIVERS OF A BUSINESS

Remember, in baseball rules, many small-small businesses do not use the formal financials, profit and loss statements (P/L's), and balance sheet, to manage the day to day operation of the business; therefore, the owners do not always keep accurate, complete, current, and correct financial records on a weekly or monthly basis. The one set of books that is primarily used to manage and run the small-small business is the checkbook. The more formal set of books are compiled only once a year because they have to file a tax return.

When it comes to the often-asked question, "Why do small-business owners not keep better books on a business?" I submit this point - how many of us can't wait to balance our checkbook every month? Most business owners did not go into business to keep books. They are too busy running the business, taking care of customers, managing employees and inventory, and taking care of the day-to-day business. The books are simply the last priority. If they did not have to file a tax return, they would not do any accounting.

However, in looking at a business' value, let's look at what we already know about an existing business. It has been there for x number of years. That means that the owner has paid a payroll every Friday for x years. The owner has paid rent every month for x years. The owner has paid the business' expenses, vendors, electric bill, etc. for x years. And the owner has made some sort of living for his or her family for x years. Wow, that is a pretty good start.

So, if I were writing a book about the value of a business, I would need to include several different chapters about things that are important and significant value drivers of a business' value in addition to the financial information. Some of these are listed below. Would you not agree with me that all of these chapters are important?

1. The LOCATION of the business

2. The FURNITURE, FIXTURES, and EQUIPMENT that help produce the company's product and/or service

3. The INVENTORY or PRODUCT that the customers buy from the business

4. The TRAINED EMPLOYEES of the business

5. The EXISTING CUSTOMER BASE that buy the company's products and services

6. The ESTABLISHED CASH FLOW sufficient to pay all of the business expenses and provide for the owner's lifestyle

7. The business' FINANCIAL RECORDS

8. The INDUSTRY ITSELF, does it have a shelf life

9. The ESTABLISHED VENDORS – SUPPLIERS RELATIONSHIP

5: VALUE DRIVERS OF A BUSINESS

10. The COMPETION

11. The possibility of SELLER FINANCING

12. WHAT YOU (the buyer) ARE GOING TO DO WITH THE BUSINESS AFTER THE SALE

Now, while you would obviously agree with me that all twelve of these things are important, following are some major disconnects from big business (football rules) and small-small business (baseball rules), reference chapter seven, the business's financial records:

A) In big business, management has a bookkeeping department and places a great deal of emphasis on current, correct, complete, and accurate financial records (the books). They use the financials in making decisions and managing the business. They also report financial news to the public and hope to sell shares of stock in their company.

B) In small-small business, the owner is the manager and normally uses "walking around" management (being there), combined with checkbook financial management in making decisions and managing the business. The formal financials are prepared only when the information is assembled (compiled), to turn over to an accountant to file a tax return. It is almost always in a "catch-up" mode and many times it is not current, correct, complete, or accurate. And most often it is based on checkbook information.

C) When you employ an accountant to protect you, or you apply for a loan at the bank - they are looking only at chapter seven, the business's financial records, for the determination of business value and earnings. They are not even taking into consideration the eleven other very important value drivers of the business. That is a mistake; however, neither you nor I can change the world or change baseball rules.

D) That is also one of the reasons why banks normally do not make small business "acquisition" loans (they do not have SECURITY in the business' assets and proven DEBT REPAYMENT ability based on the financial records. And that is why, in almost thirty years of selling small businesses, I have never once, not once, had an accountant advise a buyer to buy a small business.

If the bank and the accountant's decision is based only on chapter seven (the financial records that were basically slanted to minimize taxes), they are dealing with a false read on value and ignoring eleven out of twelve legitimate value drivers.

From a buyer's perspective, let's deal with the most important issue with and for you. What you really want to know from chapter seven is the answer to one main question, "If I buy this business," "If I buy this job," "How much can I make?" Well,

5: VALUE DRIVERS OF A BUSINESS

the information in chapter seven, put in the proper context from the seller (who knows more about this business than anyone else in the world), can give us part of that answer.

Very importantly, how much you can make is built on the following three issues:

1. How much is the present owner making (owner's benefit or SDE)

2. Less any debt service or other cost that you would have in buying the business

3. Plus what you would do to improve and grow the top line and bottom line

So let's look at chapter seven for what it does tell us. And because it is so important, let's focus an entire chapter of this book on the financials of the business. And in doing so, let's try to determine the "real" bottom line - not just the bottom line for tax purposes. And from that earnings number, try to arrive at the market value of a business. Most often, we would use some acceptable multiple of earnings (owner's benefit or SDE) - the problem is determining the real SDE and agreeing on an acceptable multiple.

Another rule of Ed's rules of buyers is that from a multiple of earnings approach to value, I have found that small-small businesses normally sell for from 2 to 4 times SDE, with the average business, over the last fifteen years, selling at 2.3 times SDE.

6

HOW DO YOU FIND THE RIGHT BUSINESS?

All right! Now you have decided that you want to go into business for yourself. You have decided that buying an existing successful business or a successful franchise is the best thing for you. You feel more comfortable about understanding what constitutes value and what you are buying (earnings/cash flow). You are more knowledgeable about why most of the things that you studied in business school do not apply to small-small business. You feel that you have a preliminary working knowledge of baseball rules. Now - how do you find a business?

Good question - the best answer is that you go to the business store. Just as if you are looking for a suit, you go to the clothing store; if you are looking for a car, you go to the car dealer; if you are looking for a house, you go to the real estate broker; if you are looking for a business, go to a business broker. The interesting thing is that most folks have never heard of a business broker. There are several reasons: confidentiality is one very important one; second, until recently, most folks thought

6: HOW DO YOU FIND THE RIGHT BUSINESS?

that having a job was the best answer to making a living; and third, there are not a lot of business brokers.

Unlike real estate, where, when the broker lists a property for sale, they want to immediately put a large FOR SALE sign on the property, list the property on several multiple listing sites, list the property on their corporate Website so everyone can do a virtual walk through of the property - in selling a business, it is entirely the opposite; you do not want ANYONE to know that the business is for sale. Not the business' employees, not their customers, not their competitors, not the vendors, not the landlord, not the banks - no one. It is important that all marketing is done confidentially. And business brokers, except in the state of Florida, normally do not co-broker deals.

Now there are several ways for you to find a business that is for sale:

1. Visit a business broker

2. Check the yellow pages for local business brokers

3. Visit pertinent Websites that list businesses for sale, normally by location, type, size, etc.

4. Check the Sunday newspaper classifieds, "Business Opportunities/Businesses for Sale"

5. Approach business owners of businesses you like; see if they want to sell, or can refer you to someone that does

6. Call or e-mail me, Ed Pendarvis, the Business Buyer's Agent, at e-mail address: edpendarvis@businessbuyersuniversity.com, or call me directly at (843) 789-4112

To say that I recommend 1 – "visit a business broker" as the best, most prudent, most efficient, smartest, and safest way for you to go would be a huge understatement. The business broker may have hundreds of businesses opportunities listed for sale in your area. And, if the broker does not have the right business for you now, he or she may be able to help you find the right business. It would most certainly broaden your process of elimination.

And just as you would contact the listing broker of a real estate property that you are interested in, I would recommend that you contact the business broker that has a business listed that you have an interest in.

Almost always, the business broker is an agent of the seller. However, while the broker works "for" the seller, he or she never works "against" the buyer. Remember, a business deal has to work for both the buyer and the seller, or it will not work for either.

My suggestion is that you take advantage of the market knowledge and professionalism of the business broker and seek his or her help in locating a good business for you. Also I can work with you, as a buyer agent or referral agent, and work with and through the seller's broker if you like. I will show you how.

Now I would always recommend a Sunbelt business broker, because I personally trained most of them, or a broker that is a

6: HOW DO YOU FIND THE RIGHT BUSINESS?

member of our industry trade group, the IBBA, or a regional affiliate of IBBA. They all have had extensive training and ascribe to the IBBA Code of Ethics. I would also be very comfortable recommending a broker that is affiliated with another franchise organization such as VR, Business Team or Murphy business brokers. They also have had extensive training to help you find and buy a business.

The designation "CBI" after a broker's name stands for "Certified Business Intermediary," which means that the broker has had at least three years' experience and has successfully studied and completed sixty-eight hours of business brokerage courses taught by the top industry professionals that are members of the industry trade group, the IBBA. And, of course, they ascribe to the IBBA Code of Ethics.

I can recommend a business broker in your area at no cost. If you would like, I could work as your buyer's agent with you and the broker, with a referral agreement with the business broker. Business brokers normally charge a 10 percent success fee commission - my referral fee would normally be 10 percent of the broker's fee paid from his or her total commission.

Contact the business broker by phone or e-mail and go and meet with him or her, just as you would meet with a doctor or lawyer. You need to establish a comfortable relationship with a local business broker. I can also help you with that. He or she will be an important part of our TEAM to help you find a good local business that is for sale. We will work together to help you Buy the Right Business (for you) Right.

7
FOCUS IS IMPORTANT

Once you start your journey of searching through the menu of businesses for sale on Websites, in newspaper classified sections, and through business brokers, and you practice your drive around process of elimination, you will begin to focus on businesses that you like and that interest you. And, just as you would look at a menu in a restaurant and out of the many selections available, all of which you could order, you narrow your possible choices to a few things. Then perhaps you ask for more information on those selections that interest you (the other items have already been eliminated by your natural process), and then ultimately you reject the items that you do not want and select the one that you do want. See - that was not so hard - was it?

Now, as we mentioned in chapter six, many of the best business opportunities are listed confidentially by business brokers. You will need to contact the broker by e-mail and/or telephone to get enough information to either eliminate that business opportunity or to look further at it. Do not be surprised

7: FOCUS IS IMPORTANT

if the broker cannot or will not give you a lot of information on the business by e-mail or over the phone. He or she has been trained not to for several reasons.

1. Confidentially - you could be an employee of that business, or a competitor (or potential competitor) just trying to get information on the business and find out if the business is for sale.

2. The broker knows that 90 percent of the time a buyer will not buy the business that they called in on (oftentimes not even the type of business that they called in on).

3. The broker knows that 90 percent of the time buyers do not know what kind of businesses they want or best serve their needs - or how to buy them.

4. The broker knows that he or she cannot really help you without taking take the time to get to know you - to know your needs and capabilities; whereas, the broker can possibly help you if he or she gets to know you and vice versa.

So be prepared to go and visit with a broker. Please be aware that business brokers almost always work as agents for sellers. They get paid by the sellers, and their legal, and fiduciary relationships are to sellers. However, they owe buyers truthfulness and "fair dealing," and most brokers never work against the best interests of the buyers. There is a very good reason for this. If the buyer doesn't buy the business, then the seller cannot sell the business and the broker does not get paid.

Also as previously mentioned, unlike real estate brokerage, there is very little co-brokering in business brokerage. Only eighteen states require a broker to have a real estate license to sell businesses. That is a major reason for this book and my position as a buyer's agent. Working as a buyer referral agent, I can help you without raising the cost. I will work with you, with the seller's broker, and with the seller to help you buy a business and my fee will be a referral fee from the business broker as a part of his or her normal fee from the seller.

Buying a business is too big and too important a decision to be made over the Internet or over the telephone. They are great portals for initial contacts that lead to a "first date"; however, just as you would not get married without going out on a first date, then building a relationship, you should most certainly not buy a business without personally getting to know everyone that you are dealing with, and then building a mutually beneficial relationship.

Because of confidentiality, a business broker simply cannot put enough complete and useful information about a business on the Website. You must meet face-to-face.

Once you start actually looking at specific business opportunities, I strongly suggest that you use another of Ed's rules of buyers. Your three main areas of focus throughout the initial stages of the process, should be:

1. FOCUS on the BUSINESS, not just on the financial information. If you do not like the business - the numbers do not matter. I believe that the most important thing is to find a business that you like and feel that you can manage and grow. Remember, any business that has been there three years or longer and is currently making someone a living could make you a living.

2. FOCUS on the TOP LINE (gross sales) not the BOTTOM LINE of the financials. Remember that the financials have been done by the business owner's accountant with the primary goal of minimizing taxes. That is what you pay your accountant for, to do everything that he or she possibly can (legally) to minimize the taxes that you have to pay. Do not be surprised if the financials show a loss for tax purposes. Much more on that later - for now remember that by Ed's rules the owner/manager of a small-small business could make from 10 percent to 20 percent of gross sales (10 percent of sales on a business doing over $1million). Of course, we will ask the owner, "How much are you making?" at the right time in the relationship.

3. FOCUS on WHAT YOU WOULD DO WITH THE BUSINESS after the sale and not just on what the

present owner/seller is doing or has done. This is most important to you. How many times have you seen a business, a restaurant, for instance (because it is such an open and visible business), actually "go out of business" and then six months later someone comes into that same location - same type of business (food service), opens back up, and "kicks the doors down" with business (same location, same business, better management).

Management plays such an important part in a business' success or failure that I recommend that you ascribe a weighting to your decision as follows:

- 30 percent of the weight of your decision to buy a business should be based on what and how the present owner has run the business for the last few years. Think about it - what can you change about how the seller has run the business for the last fifteen years? - you cannot change it a "nickel." What you can change is what you would do if you owned the business. Is that not right?

- 70 percent of the weight of your decision to buy a business should be based on "What You Would Do" after "You Owned" the business. What one, two, three, or four things would you do or change to improve and grow the business? I always ask my buyers to consider that. While you cannot change the past - you can most

7: FOCUS IS IMPORTANT

certainly change the future. And every business can be improved. You need to get started on a preliminary business plan for the next six months and for the next few years. Focus on your management plans for the business.

I have seen so many buyers, buy a business, get into the business, make several "course corrections" that make slight or major improvements (they stay open longer, they change the menu, they energize the employees, they set new goals, they advertise more, they put in a "drive thru" maybe, they build a Website, they pick up and deliver, etc.) and guess what - business gets better.

Now, in "buying the right business right," you buy the business because of the value of the potential earnings that you see going forward. However, you pay the seller for the value of the business today based on present earnings. More about that later.

SUPPLEMENT

THE FAMILY BUSINESS, THE FAMILY FARM

One of the most difficult challenges for most potential buyers of small-small businesses is to be able to get comfortable with the earnings of these businesses, relative to the financial records of the businesses. In explaining this, I prefer to use an analogy about how a family business is similar to a family farm.

Now, let's say that I had a family farm, my wife and children and I lived on the farm, and I raised corn, wheat, and peaches as my primary crops to sell. However, we also raised some chickens, cows, pigs, and a couple of horses. Neither you nor I would think that there is anything wrong with the fact that the eggs, bacon, and toast that my family and I had for breakfast came from my farm.

We did not pay retail for them and there was no accounting entry (debit or credit) recorded anywhere about breakfast. And, it was very good. When we harvested the corn crop, the wheat crop, and the peaches and sold them to the co-op or to Archer-Midland-Daniels, we got a check for each crop and that went into the farm business' bank account.

SUPPLEMENT

We got $87,300 for the corn crop, $77,920 for the wheat crop, and $64,017 for the peaches. The corn, wheat, and peaches that we "put up" for our personal consumption was not recorded anywhere. The one-acre vegetable garden that we planted for our own consumption (and a little for a contribution to the church bazaar) was not recorded in the farm's books.

We have a small roadside peach stand and one of my daughters ran that during the season and earned herself about $600 that she is using for her high school class trip to Washington, DC, later this year. And, we started off the year with ten cows; we had four calves; however, we ended up with ten cows because we ate four of them (actually, we also traded some steaks to the music teacher for some lessons for my youngest daughter), and we hosted a barbecue for my son's baseball team.

When I sat down and "compiled" my checkbook for tax purposes for the year, I showed the total income of $87,300, plus $77,920, plus $64,017 = $229,237. That is my gross sales for the year; less all of my expenses for the year. We bought a new tractor; repaired the combine; my wife got an SUV, which we sometimes use for the business; and I deducted all of the gas, repairs, and expenses for her SUV and my pickup. We repaired the fences and I took the whole family to the "Green Energy Expo" in Las Vegas with a few days' side journey to the Grand Canyon (to study the effects of erosion).

Sure enough, when my accountant got through with his work on my tax return, deducting all expenses, including depreciation, investment tax credits, and farm credits, I lost money again for the eighth straight year on the family farm.

Farming's hell, but, we like it and we had a pretty good year, all things considered.

Now be honest - most folks do not see anything wrong with the farming business' records while at the same time realizing that the farmer is busy running a farm and taking care of a family.

Well, now let's look at the folks that do not have a family farm; they have a family business - say a dry cleaners. The owner and his wife go to work each day at 6:30 a.m.; the twelve employees get there by 7:00 a.m. and they are open until 7:00 p.m. They are busy all day, taking in clothes, picking up clothes from the valet routes, processing clothes, managing employees, taking care of customers, delivering the drop-off on the valet routes and getting kids to all of the day's events.

By 7:00 p.m. they are tired and, usually, the last thing in the world that they want to do is to stay there another hour and make sure that the books balance. They have to go home, take care of the home front (including kids), and be ready to open back up tomorrow at 7:00 a.m. Let's say that today's receipts are $600 ($400 in checks, credit, and debit cards, and $200 in cash.) You put today's receipts in the bank bag and head home.

Now, sometimes, let's say that the wife says, "I am exhausted, I am too tired to cook supper (and you don't know how to cook), so let's go out to eat - you pick up the kids and go out to Applebee's or Olive Garden." Supper is $53. You stop and get gas for the car or van, $44; and sure enough, when you get home, one kid needs $20 for school tomorrow and the other

SUPPLEMENT

kid needs $20 for registration of something. Note: Kids always need $20! That never ends.

So when the business owner deposits the receipts for yesterday in the bank, the deposit is what's in the bank bag ($600, less $53, less $44, less $40 = $463). And, let's assume that the owner's son comes by the store and says, "Dad, I need some Nike shoes for practice, the owner takes $140 right out of the cash draw and goes about running his business. When the owner, using "checkbook accounting," adds up the bank deposits to get his gross sales for this month, this money never even shows up. While it went into the owner's lifestyle, it never got deposited in the bank and therefore, it never got into the business' formal financials. (And, this son works in the store on "most" Saturdays and is paid $150 cash per week.)

Then he adds up the deposits, less all of the expenses, including his delivery vehicle (a Hummer), his wife's car, and the family trip to the "green" dry cleaning trade show at Las Vegas, plus a side trip to the Grand Canyon to study how to get desert sand out of clothes. He turns his "compiled" records into his accountant and, sure enough, after all expenses - including accelerated depreciation and updated environmental mandates and job credits - he shows a loss for tax purposes. However, he's had a pretty good year at the dry cleaners and he has provided for his family and provided jobs for twelve other people. Good for him, good for his community. Good for us - small business has provided most of the net new jobs in America for the last ten years.

Both of these are good family businesses, they are making each owner a good living and, sure enough, they both show a loss for tax purposes. Welcome to the real world of small-small-family businesses. That is why I recommend that you get to know the owner of the business that you are considering and get the owner to go over the business' financials with you. Let the owner recast the numbers to show you the owner's benefit or SDE. (And remember, if the seller is using "checkbook" accounting, any cash that went into the family's lifestyle but never got deposited in the bank, does not even show up in the business' compiled financials.)

Then, when talking with the seller, as Paul Harvey used to say, "you can get the rest of the story."

8
HOW MUCH CAN I MAKE?

In the previous chapters, including the one on valuing a business, we have been building up to the answer to this very important question: "If I buy this business," "If I buy this job," "How much can I make?" Well, since so much of a business' value comes from the management, and you will be the management going forward, we have to have you, as well as the seller, in that answer.

We always say that the three most important influences on value in the real estate business (soccer rules) are (1) location, (2) location, and (3) location. In business value, that is not so. While some businesses, like a retail store or a restaurant, may depend heavily on location, a service business, like a janitorial business or landscape business, could be run out of a garage somewhere; location does not figure prominently in value.

The three most important inputs to value in a small-small business are usually (1) location (depending on the type of business), (2) the track record of the business, including the trend of sales, and (3) the management of the business. Assuming

8: HOW MUCH CAN I MAKE?

that the location is all right, and that you feel that you could manage the business, provided that the seller train and transition you properly, we will focus our approach to value on the track record - especially the financial track record.

Remember that the formula for the answer to the question, "How much can I make?" starts with (1) how much is the seller making now, (2) less the debt service created by the acquisition, and (3) what the buyer is going to do to operate, improve and grow the business going forward. Let's look first at 1, how much is a seller making now?

Well, I am going to suggest that you use three approaches to SDE. First, let's use "Ed's rules of thumb for buyers," in that we determine the annual gross sales as demonstrated by the business' financials and the tax return. This number would be the seller's representation of business' sales for the year. Applying my formula that a business that does under $1 million in gross sales could possibly make the owner/manager from 10 percent to 20 percent of gross sales (over $1 million per year, 10 percent of gross sales) - we will see if the seller's representation of owner's benefit (SDE) fits that formula. This is strictly a sanity check to get comfortable with what the seller tells you about earnings. Here is an example:

Food Service Business:

Gross Sales of "X"	100%
Less: Cost of goods sold (food costs)	(30%)
Less: Cost of labor	(30%)
Less: Rent expenses	(10%)

Less: Administration Expenses
(Advertising, insurance, Utilities) (10%)
Leaving available to owner 10% to 20%
(Dependent on management)

Of course, there is no guarantee of any earnings. That is why this is a rule of thumb; however, in my experience, it is difficult for a business to produce earnings of more than 10 - 20 percent of its gross sales.

Second, at the appropriate time, almost never on a first date, let's simply ask the only person that really knows, the seller, about how much the business is earning him and his family now. And we will also, on a first date, ask the seller why he is he selling. If this is such a good business - why is it for sale? We always want to know the seller's answer to these two questions.

Some folks seem to be nervous about asking the seller some of this information, but do not be. Please think about this. Where did you or the business broker, get virtually all of the information, financial and otherwise, on this business? Where did the accountant get the information to compile the tax return, where did the IRS get their information? All from the seller.

Third, and some folks think this is the most accurate, we will work with the seller to recast his financial records to take out the influence of trying to minimize taxes and we will "add back" certain "discretionary" expenses and perks that benefit

8: HOW MUCH CAN I MAKE?

the lifestyle of the owner and their family. This will show us the owner's benefit available to you if you operate the business in a similar manner.

In recasting the financial records of a small business, the business brokerage trade group, the IBBA, has some recommendations for processes and procedures that most good business brokers use and that I suggest that you use. First, let's obtain three years' worth of the business' most recent financial statements and tax returns. This would include P/L's (income statements) and balance sheets.

We want to see both the amount of sales and the trend of sales. We would want to see that the gross sales number on both the income statement (profit and loss) is the same number as reported to the IRS on the tax return.

Now this has never happened in Charleston, South Carolina, but I have heard that in some places, some folks do not report all of their sales. That is done to get around paying state sales taxes that are based on reported sales. Most states have a sales tax of from 6 percent to 9 percent of gross sales, due and payable on the twentieth of each month. Underreporting sales is not right and could create a liability for the business that would follow the title, even in an assets only sale. So let's deal only with reported sales in our recast.

We would start with the net sales (gross sales, less sales taxes, less returns) plus any other income that would go with the operation of the business and we then would proceed with the seller's input and representations on a line-by-line recast, or adjustment, of each expense on the financial statements. We would leave in any part of the expense that is non-discretionary (necessary to the success of the business operation). And we would back out any portion of the expense that is discretionary (not necessary for the success of the business but does benefit the lifestyle of the owner and/or owner's family.)

According to IBBA recast rules, we would back out all expenses of the depreciation and all of the expenses of amortization (these are non-cash expenses). We would back out interest expenses (you would have a different interest expense, unless you are taking over the existing debt). We would back out personal auto expenses, insurance, travel expenses, cell phone and tech expenses that are perks and family benefits - however, are not necessary for the business' operation. Hence they are discretionary expenses. That adjusted amount of money in each line would be added back to the income (or loss) shown on the financial statements (pretax). We would back out any family members' benefits that are not producing employees of the business.

Any and all lines need to be normalized to adjust for any one-time or nonrecurring income and/or expense so that you get the best and most realistic picture of the true earnings, or SDE, that you should have available to you if you purchased the business. And, assuming that you would continue to do about the same amount of sales and keep the same nondiscretionary expenses, that SDE is what you should have available to pay any cost of purchasing the business and provide a lifestyle for you.

I usually recast the income statement (P/L) pretax, because (1) your tax situation may be entirely different and (2) the

8: HOW MUCH CAN I MAKE?

seller's tax return may be influenced by other things such as a "carry forward losses" and/or special accelerated tax treatments available only once.

So, armed with the information provided by the seller, perhaps through an accountant or broker, you now have the base answer for the question, "How much could I make if I bought this business" (how much the seller is making now). Take out any expenses of your purchase of the business and, very importantly, add in any proposed improvements and/or growth that you would provide in gross sales and/or SDE and you have your answer.

The second part of the formal financial records (in addition to the P/L's or income statement) is the balance sheet. Whereas, in small-small businesses, the P/L's are the "compiled" records of sales, expenses, and earnings, over a specific period of operations (usually a month or a year); the Balance Sheet is a "snap shot" of the assets, liabilities, and equity of the business, on a specific date, say December 31, 2008. The problem is using allowable, acceptable, legal accounting practices the balance sheet is oftentimes not appropriate to use. It may give you a false read.

For instance, the business may have F, F, and E of $400,000, depreciated for tax purposes down to $35,000 after six years. That is an artificial number. If you ask the seller how much furniture, fixtures, and equipment are in the business, the seller would probably say about $350,000, but the balance sheet shows $35,000. That may be a huge false read, based on the influence of tax laws.

Also, the year-end inventory may not reflect how much paid for inventory is in the business (garbage in - garbage out). I normally do not consider the balance sheet in a small-small business, except for information purposes.

Remember Ed's rules of buyers that sales drive value. So to make sense and work for you, the business has to make enough sales to make enough money to pay its debt service and make you a living, or you have to believe that you can make that happen with your management. Sales are found on the P/L and income statement, not on the balance sheet.

Now, over the years I have sold a lot of businesses that were not making any money (SDE); however, the prospective buyer felt that he or she could buy that existing business opportunity and build a more successful business on the existing base that already had a known name and location, trained employees, an established customer base, and existing cash flow (perhaps just not enough) and make the business more successful. The fact that it was not making a lot of SDE certainly influenced the price of the business; however, it had a value to the buyer who bought the business and built on that existing base. Incidentally, when I bought the other folks out of Sunbelt Business Brokers in Charleston years ago, it was losing money because of management issues. However, the existing business already had a known name, an office location, trained brokers, existing listings, a telephone number, and a yellow page ad. I felt that those things had value, as opposed to starting up a new business. Fortunately, we were right.

8: HOW MUCH CAN I MAKE?

We bought the existing business with negotiated terms and conditions that worked for both buyer and seller and operated successfully in Charleston, South Carolina, until 1993 when we started growing through franchising Sunbelt. We opened offices regionally at first - then around the United States and the world.

9
FINANCING, THE "MOTHER'S MILK" OF BUYING AND SELLING

Financing is the "mother's milk" of buying and selling most any big-ticket item. Just as we normally have to finance a house, a car, a boat, a college education, or any other large purchase, we have to obtain financing to purchase a business. And financing the purchase of a business is almost always a challenge; however, as in all challenges, there are tried-and-true ways to accomplish our objectives. We shall look at several different alternatives.

In buying a house, the financing is normally done by mortgage bankers that will loan up to 90 percent of the value of the house (owner occupied) based on contract value and/or comparable values established by the sale of similar properties in that subdivision or area. The loan is normally for thirty years and it is secured by the "good faith" (personal signatures) of the purchasers and a first mortgage security interest on the real estate that is being purchased. The mortgage banker services the

9: FINANCING, THE "MOTHER'S MILK" OF BUYING AND SELLING

loan and then bundles this loan with other similar securities and sells the note to the secondary market, perhaps to investors or to Fannie Mae or Freddie Mac (quasi-governmental agencies that help make a market in residential home loans). The mortgage banker gets the discounted proceeds and makes more loans. Their money is not tied up for thirty years on the loan.

To qualify for the loan, the buyer had to have reasonable credit (usually, above a 625 credit score) and verified income or proof of employment that showed the necessary cash flow available to service the debt and provide a living for the buyer and his or her family. And, usually, the house payments could not exceed about 33 percent of the total family income.

In buying an automobile, the financing could be done by a bank or the financing arm of the automobile company itself set up to help the company sell cars - for instance, Ford Motor Credit, GMAC Finance, Chrysler Credit, etc. They would make loans to finance the purchase of their cars, sometimes in spite of some buyers' credit issues, as long as they had debt repayment ability through proof of employment. The loan amount was normally amortized over a five–seven-year period at an interest rate set by the marketplace. Oftentimes, to help promote sales, they would offer 0 percent interest.

The automobile title was the security as well as the good faith of the borrower through personal signatures. Since all states require annual vehicle registration and insurance, the lender had identifiable security and verified debt repayment ability. Once the loan was paid off, the title was sent to the owner.

The average range of value of Main Street businesses is $300,000–$400,000. Most potential buyers have from $50,000–$100,000 available as a potential investment in a down payment. That obviously means that on a $300,000 business acquisition, someone has to finance the balance of $200,000–$250,000.

And, in buying a business, we have an unusual set of circumstances. We are buying an ongoing economic entity that requires management to make or keep the assets of this business valuable, viable, and "cash flowing" in the marketplace. Whereas the real estate and even the car have somewhat of an acceptable market-driven value regardless of your management - the business value is very dependent on management for its continued success. That makes it a real challenge for banks to make a loan on a business acquisition.

Whereas, the existing operating business' sales may be sufficient to pay the expense of operating the business and produce a lifestyle for the owner, what happens to the cash flow and the value of the assets if the business closes? If the owner were to close an operating business (like a restaurant or dry cleaners), the market value of those same assets (furniture, fixtures, equipment, inventory, goodwill, trademarks/trade names) might go down to 5–10 percent of their original value.

For all these reasons banks do not usually make small business "acquisition" loans. The reason that banks can say they make small business loans is that sometimes you can get a loan, or lease, on new equipment, or perhaps in buying a franchise, the franchisor may have financing available on

9: FINANCING, THE "MOTHER'S MILK" OF BUYING AND SELLING

a "start-up package," somewhat similar to the automobile financing arrangement. And, banks do make small-business loans on receivables (factoring) to folks that are already in business and that they have a relationship with.

You see, they have the existing customer's business' bank records - they can see that the business always keeps a positive bank balance, that they pay their bills, that they have the cash flow available to repay a loan for expansion, inventory, or an operating loan. So they do make loans to existing clients with a track record of successful management and they are not just looking at the business' financials - they have their bank records. Almost 80 percent of bank loans and SBA (Small Business Administration) loans are to their existing bank customers.

That is why it is oftentimes confusing when banks say, "We are the small-business lender in _____ town." However, when you make an application, they will normally not lend you the money to acquire or start up a business for two reasons that actually have very little to do with you and your credit.

1. SECURITY: The bank has to have security for the loan (security, meaning, in a worst-case scenario, what assets could the bank seize, take back to the marketplace, and get their money back in sixty–ninety days) and, as mentioned earlier, the assets of a closed business have little, if any, value in the marketplace.

2. PROVEN DEBT REPAYMENT ABILITY: The bank has to see where the debt repayment is coming from, and

since you are depending on the business' future earnings to provide for repayment, plus give you enough income for your personal expenses (lifestyle), the financials of the business have to show the available cash flow to accomplish that. They seldom do, since most often the focus of the formal financial records is to minimize taxes. (Many businesses actually show a loss for tax purposes.) And the bank would like to have at least 125 percent cash flow to loan payment coverage.

Note: Bankers will always say, "We are the small business lender." They are sincere and they will always take your application [bankers are equal opportunity application takers - the VPs have to have something to do]; however, they will always ask you to bring in the last three years financials of the business that you are buying ...caution - never stand in front of the banker when he or she is looking at the financials; the banker will probably throw up all over the floor.

And do not be surprised that after some effort, many requests for more information, and several weeks of processing, the banker says that the bank cannot make the loan because the banker cannot get comfortable with the security and cannot find the proven debt repayment ability for the loan and a lifestyle for you. Do not give up; perhaps they would consider making the loan with an SBA guarantee.

The banks may be able to solve part of the security issue if you are able to get a loan guarantee from the SBA that secures 70 to 90 percent of the loan amount with a guarantee

9: FINANCING, THE "MOTHER'S MILK" OF BUYING AND SELLING

from the United States government. Most lenders can work with the SBA and approximately 20 percent of small business transactions are financed, at least in part, by the lender with an SBA guarantee. The lender then services the loan and, like the real estate mortgage banker, they may discount the loan to the secondary market, the security market.

One note, the SBA normally requires a personal signature of your promise to make the loan payments as agreed, a security interest in all of the assets of the business being acquired, and the additional security of a second or third mortgage on your primary house. They also know that the assets of a closed business have little, if any, value in the marketplace and they want to get paid.

So, if the SBA and/or banks make loans in only a small percent of business acquisitions, how can we get the financing that we need to buy a business? The market value is $300,000 and we still have only $50,000–$100,000 to put down on the purchase. Someone has to finance the purchase or we will not be able to buy the business.

Yes, that is true. And, to get the loan, that lender has to be comfortable with the exact same real issues with the loan that the banker had: (1) security and (2) debt repayment ability, plus lifestyle for the buyer coming out of the cash flow of the business. Let's look at both issues.

Would you not agree with me that the best and most logical lender is the seller of the business? Unlike the banker, who cannot manage the business if something happens to the buyer (the bank closes the business in forced liquidation and gets 5–10 percent of the loan, maybe); the seller has been successfully managing the business for years. The seller knows the employees, the customers, the equipment, the inventory, the industry, etc., so in a worst-case scenario, the seller could take the business back as security and it really is valuable security (I know the seller does not want to, but he or she could).

How about 2, debt repayment ability and a lifestyle for the buyer coming out of the available cash flow of the business? Forget about what the formal set of financials that were done to minimize taxes do not show - look at them for what they do show and tell you. The gross sales and the trend of sales and what the seller represents about the owner's benefit, or cash flow. And, who knows more about the true cash flow of the business than the seller? In fact, I will submit to you that the seller is the only one that truly knows what the real cash flow of the business is.

Let's ask the seller to finance the business. Now, the seller probably would rather not; he or she would prefer that you find the money somewhere else and just pay the $300,000 to the seller at closing. However, if the banks won't do it, the SBA won't do it, you, the buyer, only have $50,000–$100,000 to put down, then the seller has a decision to make.

Would the seller rather not sell the business and keep getting up at 5:30 a.m. to open the business or would the seller rather sell the business to "these nice people that want my business, who are investing everything they have to buy my business"? Why not let them get up at 5:30 a.m. every morning to open the business and let them pay the seller 6 or 7 percent

9: FINANCING, THE "MOTHER'S MILK" OF BUYING AND SELLING

on a secured loan for five to seven to ten years on the balance of the purchase price? Where else could the seller get 7 percent on his or her money in today's market?

To me, seller financing makes so much sense for both seller and buyer. The number one reason is that it helps sell the business for a fair price. But, it also gives the buyer a level of comfort that the seller, who knows more about this business than anyone else in the world, is willing to invest in the "go forward" success of the business. The seller still has some skin in the game.

The seller is putting $$$$ where his or her mouth is, saying, "This is a good business. The cash flow is here to make you a living and pay me. I believe that you can be successful in this business and I will help you," because, "I want you to pay me the money that you owe me - my family and I are counting on it."

I am a strong believer in seller financing. In fact, I teach a workshop at IBBA conferences on the advantages of seller financing. It helps to bridge the leap of faith between the seller and the buyer. It certainly adds credibility to the seller's warranties and representations. Many times it is the best, and only way to get financing for the fair market value of the business.

Oftentimes, you could end up with a combination of financing options that make the deal work. These could include a certain amount down by the purchaser, a first-position loan by a bank or other lender with or without an SBA guarantee, and a second-position security interest by the seller. Other options include balloon payments, earn-outs, delayed payments, seasonal adjustments, etc.

Additional financing options can come from the buyer's friends and family or others that will help you get started by enhancing your down payment ability and making you a loan or gift because of their relationship with and belief in you.

One word of advice - the friends and family are helping you because of their relationship with you - not the value of the business; however, my recommendation is that you treat this loan just like you would a loan from a bank or other investor. You should have a note, signed by you with repayment terms and conditions spelled out so that everyone knows what to expect. That allows you to keep a good relationship with your friends and family.

One way, two ways, or some way; we have to put a deal together that works and that is acceptable by both sellers and buyers. And, it has to be a deal that works for everyone...a win-win-win deal. And always remember, the cash flow (SDE) has to be enough to pay any debt service and still provide enough owner benefit to provide for the buyer's lifestyle. Or you have to feel comfortable that you can make that happen under your improved management of the business.

Can we put together acceptable financing to buy a business that we like and feel that we can manage? We'll see.

10
NEGOTIATE WITH A BUYER/SELLER-FRIENDLY OFFER

Negotiations play a major role in selling and buying all businesses. In big business, part of the payment of the purchase price of a company that is purchased by a publicly traded company may be through acquiring a company's shares of stock rather than normal currency, defined as cash - "American." The value of the company's shares of stock are set by the marketplace and, as we have seen, they can vary greatly. The management of the acquiring company is staying in place after the acquisition and they usually have ongoing relationships with lenders. This avenue of financing is not available to private, small businesses. The buyer does not have stock that has acknowledged market value. And normally the new buyer of the small business will be a new owner who will have to develop his or her own new banking relationships.

In real estate transactions, normally banks or mortgage bankers may lend up to 90 percent of the purchase price of an

10: NEGOTIATE WITH A BUYER/SELLER-FRIENDLY OFFER

owner-occupied house for thirty years, based on government and market-based interest rates, and based on comparable value of similar houses in that area. The only things that matter are (1) What's the down payment? (2) What are the monthly payments? and (3) Does my spouse like the house? There are normally not a lot of negotiations in buying a house unless you are in a seriously overbuilt area. If every house in the neighborhood is selling at from $350,000–$450,000, I can pretty well tell you that what a normal house in that area would sell for and the primary reason is the availability of 90 percent financing. The financing makes the real estate market work because most Americans do not have $350,000–$450,000 in "Hip National Bank."

Let me ask you to think about something. If every house in the subdivision were selling for $350,000–$450,000 and there were no bank or mortgage financing...what would a house in that subdivision sell for? More? Less? Will it sell? Well, I submit to you that it would sell for what the market says it will sell for - based on what a willing seller and a willing buyer could work out and price, terms, and conditions that work for and are agreeable to both seller and buyer. They would probably arrive at price, terms, and conditions through negotiations, and the amount of the all-important down payment would be derived at by how much the buyer had and could put down, rather than just "how much the seller wants." The buyer cannot pay more down that he or she has. Guess what - that is exactly the marketplace that we are in when dealing with small-small business.

Another thing that differentiates the acquisition of small-small businesses and big businesses, and even real estate, is the role that negotiations play in arriving at a successful transaction. This is particularly true, on several levels, for folks that have been raised in the United States of America.

For our purposes, I will call folks that were born and raised in the US of A, "Older Americans," not necessarily by age in years, but by cultural bias. And, I will call folks that have moved to the USA from somewhere else in the world (this generation), "New Americans." Older Americans' and new Americans' comfort levels with price negotiations in our shopping habits and our approach to negotiations are vastly different.

You see, Older Americans have a cultural bias against negotiations when we shop for products and/or services. Not that that is good or bad - it is just so. When you go through the checkout line in a grocery store - Walmart, Kmart, Home Depot - or pay for gas, or check out of a restaurant or hotel - "zip, zip, zip," they run the barcode through the register. That is the price; therefore, that is the cost to you; therefore, that is the value. We either pay the price - or - we do not buy the item.

We would not dream of stopping the checkout line in a grocery store when the register rings up $130.28 and say, "Let me ask you something, would you take $80 cash for these groceries"? If you do not believe me about that, try that the next time that you are in a checkout line with your children next to you. They will very quietly move away from you and think to themselves..."I hope nobody knows that that's my daddy."

10: NEGOTIATE WITH A BUYER/SELLER-FRIENDLY OFFER

NICE FOLKS DON'T NEGOTIATE - they either pay the price or they don't buy the product or service.

About the only place that Older Americans are comfortable negotiating on price is at a flea market, a garage sale, or when buying an automobile. And every time that they take a survey on what folks don't like the most about buying an automobile, guess what the number one answer is? It's the hassle of negotiations. Older Americans are not good negotiators. We are uncomfortable and do not like negotiating; we normally either pay the price, or we do not buy the item.

Not so with New Americans. They have a cultural bias toward negotiations. From their perspective, why would you not try to get a better deal on everything? Everything is negotiable, their entire world of buying things in their old country is based on everyday negotiations. They bring those traits, skills, and experiences here.

For instance, I will have a convenience store for sale and the seller, an Older American, is asking $400,000, all cash, for the business assets, subject to the lease assignment being transferred to the new buyer. Based on the earnings of the business, this asking price may be appropriate or it may be a little high - either way, that is the asking price.

When I confidently show the business to an Older American buyer, who has only $60,000 in savings for a down payment, he does not make an offer. Even though he may like the business otherwise, he says that he thinks that $400,000 is too much for the business, so no offer - no negotiations = no sale.

Now comes a potential buyer from South Korea (or India, or Vietnam, or the Middle East, etc.), a New American, and he has $60,000 in savings for a down payment. He likes the business; he summarily dismisses the $400,000 asking price, which he thinks is too much for the business; however, he offers the seller $60,000 for the business. Of course, the seller is upset and says absolutely not.

So the New American goes away for about two weeks, looks at other business opportunities, decides that he still likes the convenience store, so he comes back and changes his offer to $60,000 down and a seller-financed note for $100,000. The seller again says absolutely not. The buyer goes away again.

About three weeks later, you go by the store and there is a new owner in the store, a New American, from Korea. And, I will guarantee you that he did not pay $400,000 cash for the store. Through negotiations, back and forth, a seller that wanted and/or needed to sell and a buyer that wanted to buy got a deal together that worked for both parties.

When the Older American heard the asking price of $400,000, he decided not to buy it because he thought that the price was too high. When the New American heard the asking price of $400,000, he only heard one thing: "I WANT TO SELL." He figured, "You want to sell - I would like to buy, LET'S DANCE!"

We can learn a lot from New Americans, as, of course, they can from us. They work hard and negotiate hard; however, they do buy businesses to provide a slice of the American Dream of owning your own business, for themselves and their families.

10: NEGOTIATE WITH A BUYER/SELLER-FRIENDLY OFFER

They bring those negotiating skills to America and that has served them well when it comes to buying small-small businesses. Almost 24 percent of small-small-businesses sales are made by New Americans. They make offers and they negotiate workable prices, terms, and conditions. Good for them - good for us.

So, when you see a business that you like and feel that you could manage, do not be afraid to make an offer, based on price, terms, and conditions that make sense to you and that work for you. We just might be able to put a deal together (nothing beats a failure like a try).

Consider this - the down payment has to be an amount of cash that you could put down on the business at closing and still have a little working capital available - no matter what the seller is asking. In small-small business that is usually 20 percent to 50 percent of the purchase price. Normally, the balance is financed by the seller for five, seven, or ten years at an interest rate of 6–7 percent.

When you make an offer, keep the deal as simple as possible to start with; it can get complicated (all the more reason to start off simple). $_____purchase price, $_____down payment, $_____ balance financed by seller for _____ months at _____ percent interest, monthly payments of $_____, beginning _____ days after closing, and the business will have the normal level of owned inventory of $_____ at closing. All equipment is to be in good working order and all licenses in place. The seller keeps the cash in the business and the accounts receivable and accounts payable. The seller will work with the buyer to obtain an acceptable lease or lease transfer.

Many times we will end up with a deal that is one-third down; one-third financed by a third-party lender, perhaps with an SBA guaranty; and one-third financed by the seller in a second security position. Sometimes the seller will insist that he wants to be in a first security position and I have to relate one of the absolute rules of nature - "The Big Dog Don't Eat Last!" And the bank is always "The Big Dog." The bank always wants to be first or they won't play.

And, remember some more of Ed's rules of buyers;

1. Take the time to look at the business market in your community, look at businesses that interest you and that you feel that you could run and that you would be pleased to say you owned.

2. Take the time to visit personally with a business broker that has businesses listed in your market (this is far too important for just Internet or telephone contact).

3. Take the time to look at and visit incognito any business opportunities that you are interested in, get a feel for the business without anyone, including the owner, knowing that you are a potential buyer (obviously, there are some businesses that you cannot just "visit," like a manufacturing business. You would in that case need an appointment - perhaps after hours, and always

10: NEGOTIATE WITH A BUYER/SELLER-FRIENDLY OFFER

visit the owner with the broker, if the business is listed through the broker, who can be very helpful).

4. Always meet personally with the seller, perhaps after hours (and with spouses) to get to know the seller, to hear the seller's story, including why is he selling and how much he thinks that you could make owning the business (this meeting is very important for a "gut feeling" about the business and the seller). It is also the best opportunity to make a good first impression on the seller; who you want to like you - remember, he is selling his "baby," a business that he built and managed and that has made him and his family a living for years; you may even want the seller to be your banker (whether the seller wants to or not).

5. Never do any face-to-face negotiating with the seller on the first visit (if there is a broker involved, all negotiations should go through the broker).

6. You should already know if you like the business (through a process of elimination) and you should have the preliminary financial information available to you as furnished by the seller, perhaps through the broker, that represents the gross sales, what the seller represents that he is making (SDE). You can see if that fits, based on my 10/20 percent rule (subject to your verification through due diligence if we get that far).

7. You know how much you need to make a year to provide a minimum "lifestyle" for you and your family; you know how much you are comfortable coming up with in a down payment (take a deep breath), you are ready to make an offer, subject to absolute "walk away" clauses on a contingency contract.

8. Never start off with a full price offer (you can always come up).

9. Never take yourself out of cash with your down payment (you have to have some working capital, plus house payments, car payments, etc.), and remember, the monthly payments on the debt service (terms and conditions) have to come out of the reported SDE, still leaving you enough money to provide your minimum family lifestyle,

10. Never pay all cash at closing; allow for a little "what if" money (to allow for a no-surprises training and transition of the business). If you do end up with an all cash deal, I suggest that you place from $10,000 to $20,000 in the closing attorney's escrow account for sixty to ninety days to ensure a smooth transition. This provides some ability to offset any surprises - otherwise the hold back amount is released to the seller after the hold back period.

10: NEGOTIATE WITH A BUYER/SELLER-FRIENDLY OFFER

11. Always ask the seller to finance at least part of the purchase price (you have a lender that can really help you with business issues, and you sleep better knowing that the seller, who knows more about this business than anyone else in the world, has money invested in your continued success).

12. Make any offer contingent on the following:

    A) Buyer review and approval of the financials of the business
    B) Buyer review and approval of the terms and conditions of an acceptable lease
    C) Buyer/Seller agreement on an acceptable training and transition period for new management
    D) Buyer/Seller agreement on an acceptable industry non-compete agreement
    E) Buyer being able to obtain any necessary financing at acceptable terms to the buyer
    F) All equipment to be in good working order at the time of closing
    G) The normal level of sellable inventory will be in the business at closing

13. Make an offer accompanied by a small refundable deposit (I recommend $1,000) to be held in an escrow account with the broker or an attorney (never the seller, or the seller's attorney), pending getting to an acceptable

negotiated offer contract, and subject to due diligence. Once you are at an acceptable contract, and you are satisfied with your due diligence you can "step up" the deposit to $5,000 or more, if necessary.

14. All offers should be in writing with a requested response from the seller of from three days to a week.

15. Always keep the horse in front of the cart; let's make an offer and at least see if we can negotiate an acceptable price, terms, and conditions with the seller, subject to due diligence, before we spend a lot of time and money with accountants and attorneys. Why do due diligence at the full asking price, all cash, if you do not want to pay that much, if you don't have that much cash, and a bank will not lend you that much? If we cannot work out something that makes sense and works for you, the buyer, and the seller, all things considered, we will have to look at other opportunities.

Over the years I have seen some amazing deals come about because of a positive relationship being built between the seller and the buyer. I have seen sellers that insisted that they would absolutely not do any owner financing who financed 60–70 percent of the selling price (after they met and liked the buyer, and the market had shown them that no one could get financing on that business.) And the buyer made a sincere offer - in writing, saying, " I would like to buy your business,

10: NEGOTIATE WITH A BUYER/SELLER-FRIENDLY OFFER

and I will give you most of my life savings as a down payment, if you will just finance the balance of the sale."

Through honest, managed negotiations we learn what level of down payment is acceptable and necessary. I have helped buyers uncover and identify additional down payment ability and/or third party financing. We can use pick-up payments, balloon payments, inventory adjustments or assume "in place" financing. There are a lot of creative ways to get the seller and buyer to their goal line.

The main issue is often the down payment. Small-small business is almost always a down payment-driven business. And the most important ratio that I try to arrive at for the buyer is a 1:1 ratio on "cash invested to annual return" in a down payment.

Think about this; if you can buy a business with a down payment of say $70,000, and the business' owner's benefit, or SDE, pays the monthly debt service for the acquisition and still makes you $70,000 per year for your lifestyle - that is a 100 percent return on your money every year for the rest of your life, and the business is paying for itself.

If you can buy a business for $50,000 or $100,000 down payment; have the cash flow (SDE, SDCF) to pay the debt service, and you can make $50,000 or $100,000 per year for your lifestyle…that is a 100 percent return on your money. Where else could you make 100 percent on your money? And, you can grow the business from there.

So let's see if we can find a business that you like, meet with the seller and start the dance by making a "Buyer/Seller-

Friendly Offer" that makes sense and works for you. (And, also that protects you.) Then we will see what the seller comes back with (in writing) in a counteroffer and we will have a much better idea of our chances of putting a deal together that works for everyone.

"You can do it," as the Home Depot says, and "I can help."

11

DUE DILIGENCE - (NEVER FUN AND EASY)

Well, let's say that we now have reached a contract with an acceptable price, terms, and conditions between the seller and the buyer of a small-small business, subject to the contingencies. Or, it could be that we are close enough to a contract agreement to go ahead with the due diligence necessary to make a final decision to buy the business, remove the contingencies and set up to close the transaction.

Normally, through negotiations, we have arrived at a spot where the seller is getting less than he wanted and the buyer is paying more than she wanted; so both parties feel that they have "given some" and they may feel just a little "stretched." While getting here took some maneuvering, perhaps some give and take, both sides get tired of negotiating after one, two, or three steps. So, hopefully, we are close to a workable deal - still, subject to the buyer's due diligence.

11: DUE DILIGENCE - (NEVER FUN AND EASY)

Here is where former President, Ronald Reagan's wise adage, "Trust, but verify," becomes so appropriate. The buyer simply wants to verify that the information, as provided by the seller, is correct and accurate. This is a pivotal point in the relationship between the seller and the buyer. And it is very important that the due diligence process be handled properly or the whole deal could come unraveled.

It is important to note that the buyer is not telling the seller that he does not trust her. He is only following a necessary process to convey that he is taking the information that the seller has provided on the business as the correct information; however, he does need to verify it before he risks his life savings on buying the business. In fact, through this process he will also be doing final due diligence on his business plan for the business "after the sale."

And, keep in mind that due diligence, by its very nature, is designed to both verify information and to look for problems (and there are always some problems and opportunities that come out and present themselves during due diligence).

While the buyer is responsible for his own due diligence, I always recommend that he put a team together, including himself (the buyer), the seller, any business broker that may be involved, an accountant to review the financials, and an attorney to represent him in the closing (and perhaps to file any needed organizational papers, such as forms for incorporation, a partnership or LLC, at the right time).

Now, a professional airline pilot always uses a written checklist, no matter how many times he takes off and lands, to make sure that he "checks off" each and every important step and that he is ready to go or to land. Well, just like the pilot, you will need to make yourself a due diligence checklist that basically sets out each and every step that I mention in this chapter. (A checklist is found in the appendix/forms section). And while I recommend that you assign certain tasks and duties to each member of your team in their areas of expertise, the ultimate decision to "go-or-not-to-go" is up to the pilot, you.

Many times in a small-small-business deal, we would recommend using an escrow agency, as they do in California, or an escrow attorney, as they do in many other states to manage the closing process.

Now, while no attorney calls him or herself an escrow attorney, in this case one may serve in an escrow capacity to prepare and manage the closing. This attorney does not represent either the seller or the buyer; the attorney simply checks the title of the business assets, prepares the closing papers (asset purchase agreement, bill of sale, notes, security agreements, bulk sales, etc.), and manages the closing process. If you use the services of an escrow agency or escrow attorney, the buyer and the seller could split that fee fifty-fifty (usually from $1,000 to $3,000, depending on the size of the deal).

And, if you use an escrow attorney to close, you should have "your attorney" review the documents before the closing, advise you on any recommended changes in the documents and coordinate any changes with you and the escrow attorney. Your attorney, or an escrow attorney, could help you set up a

11: DUE DILIGENCE - (NEVER FUN AND EASY)

legal structure or incorporation papers for you to take title to the business' assets.

Oftentimes, attorneys are more used to being "advocates of" or "representatives of" either the seller or the buyer, as a client. That is fine except that in the position as advocate for one side or the other, the lawyer can sometimes make the deal become far more adversarial than necessary. And, please understand this - the lawyer's primary job as advocate is not to get the deal done, it is to protect his or her client. And, the only way to completely protect a client from a business deal is to not do the deal."

SIDEBAR: If I were your lawyer and I wanted to protect you from ever having to go through the pain and agony and human tragedy of a divorce, my advice would be, "Don't get married." Or, if you insist on getting married, for goodness sakes, let me draw up a prenuptial agreement to protect you.

WOW! I don't know of anything that would kill romance quicker than that. "Sweetheart, before we go out to a wonderful and romantic dinner tonight, I have a little agreement that my lawyer drew up, and if you will, please take a minute and go over it and then...sign right here." Probably, the only person "going out" will be you.

And, in a business deal, sometimes, the seller's lawyer and the buyer's lawyer feel that they have to try to renegotiate the deal's price, terms, and conditions on behalf of their clients, even when everyone has agreed on them. Hence the phrase that sometimes, "Lawyers are deal killers."

Actually, good lawyers and good accountants are good dealmakers and they help make the deal happen. However, you have to understand where the accountant and/or lawyer are coming from and what role they play in the transaction. That is another reason that I suggest the services of a business broker whose job it is to deal with all of the players and help find solutions to problems and get the deal done.

In the case of an accountant reviewing the financials for you, be prepared for more questions than answers. And, please realize that you have given the accountant a very difficult assignment. You have asked the accountant to review and verify the financial information, including the owner's benefit (SDE), and you have given him or her the business' financial records that have normally been compiled by the seller and processed by another accountant with the goal of minimizing income taxes. They have not been prepared to demonstrate cash flow. (And, remember, you pay taxes based only on profits...no profits = no taxes.)

Do not be surprised when your accountant, just like the banker, says, "Mr. Buyer, based on what I see in these compiled financials - while I am not going to say professionally, "do not buy the business," I am most certainly NOT going to say professionally, "that you should buy the business."

It is a good idea to get your accountant to talk with the seller's accountant or to the seller to explain any questions and/or issues that your accountant may have. Oftentimes the only way for you to get comfortable with the seller's warranties and representations about the earnings of the business is to have a

11: DUE DILIGENCE - (NEVER FUN AND EASY)

personal meeting back with the seller to go over the financial information with the seller - one on one.

Ask the seller to explain the recast numbers. Many times the only thing that an accountant knows about the business is the information provided by the seller. And accountants dealing with their client's small business' compiled statements normally deal with former President Bill Clinton's wise adage of "Don't Ask - Don't Tell." They have not verified any of the numbers and they say so. Therefore, let's look at the financials for what they do tell us.

First, focus on the actual gross sales of the business for the last three years. Apply the 10 percent to 20 percent rule of thumb for possible owner's benefit. Does it "fit' with the seller's representation? What is the trend of the sales? (And, "the trend is your friend.") Normally, the best indication of future events is what has happened in the most recent past and what is happening now. Many businesses obviously would have a drop in sales over this last year because of the most challenging economic environment in seventy-five years - let's allow for that. However, we still have to make a living and pay the debt service out of SDE. What are the most recent tends?

Next, go over the cost of goods sold to look for any changes or possible changes in products, services, or vendors that may be positive or negative. Ask the seller's opinion on the prospects for continued balance in that area, relative to sales.

Next, go through the expenses, line by line, with the seller and have the seller explain any recast adjustments to give you an explanation of discretionary expenses that are added back to owner's benefit (SDE).

Review the depreciation line to see if "all" of the depreciation can be added back or if some FF and E has to be replaced soon (requiring a major capital expense). Make sure that you "normalize" the income and expenses to adjust for any unusual, or one-time, income and expense. Also, take out any non-business-related income and expenses that will not be a part of the business that you are buying.

You may wish to see the seller's checkbook relative to the business, or to review bank statements or paid receipts or invoices. In essence, you are simply trying to answer the main question. "If I buy this business, how much can I make?" And the foundation for that answer begins with, "How much is the seller making now?"

Once we are satisfied that we are in a "ballpark" on SDE, and we feel that we can take over the business and have sufficient cash flow to pay the debt service and provide a lifestyle for ourselves and our family, let's review the other major assets of the business.

How about the employees? Have you not heard the statement that at 5:00 p.m. every day, the main assets of a business walk right out of the door? There is some truth in that. Let's ask the seller to go over the jobs, title, experience, longevity, salary, attitude, and expectations of at least the "key" employees. Are there any written agreements, perks, insurance, vehicles, promotions and/or bonuses due or expected?

11: DUE DILIGENCE - (NEVER FUN AND EASY)

You should get a copy of the existing lease, assuming that the business is in leased property, and review it. Most every lease has a canticle in it "that the premises cannot be assumed, let, sublet, or assigned without the written permission of the landlord. Sometimes, when I am dealing with sellers or brokers, they will say that the lease is not a problem. The only thing that I know for sure is that they have not talked to the landlord yet. The lease is always a problem. However, properly handled, we can get it transferred or assigned with the landlord's approval.

Please be prepared to provide the landlord with your personal and business biography, a personal or business financial statement, perhaps a credit report (if asked for), and a brief business plan for the business that you are buying. They will usually work with you and the seller because they want a tenant to "stay and pay." Allow two weeks to a month to get a new lease if your landlord is not local.

Review any and all "in-place" contracts, pending contracts or bids, lines of credit, and/or agreements with customers, suppliers, vendors, employees, insurance companies, permitting agencies, license agreements, regulatory agencies, or any other possible obligations for the continuous successful operation of your business. Many of these things may be canceled or become invalid upon the transfer of ownership of the business and they have to be applied for or renewed.

Is the business a franchise? If so, you are actually dealing with two sellers. Obtain and review the franchise documents including the current UFOC (uniform franchise offering circular) of the franchise. And, be aware, that only the franchisor (the parent company), not the franchisee (the individual franchisee-seller), can actually sell you a franchise. The seller (franchisee) can sell you his or her rights to the business and franchise; but only with the agreement of the franchisor. Oftentimes there is a transfer fee involved and certain requirements for training before a new license agreement or franchise agreement is issued to you, the buyer. Allow two weeks to two months for a franchise agreement transfer and training. Your ongoing relationship will be with the franchisor.

Are there any equipment leases or rental agreements that are going to be assumed by you, the buyer? Are they capital leases (lease-to-own), or are they operating leases (you never own the equipment)? What are the terms - are they needed, can they be canceled?

Again, what we are trying to do is to minimize surprises. As far as is possible we want to know what we are buying and that we will be getting what we think that we are buying. We need to make sure that this business, with continued good management, meets our expectations.

Allow at least two weeks, to a month, for due diligence after you get the information and make sure that you write down any questions and "ask the seller," who knows more about this business than anyone else in the world, for an explanation for any things that you do not feel comfortable with or about. After all, if the seller is going to finance at least part of the purchase price - he or she has a strong vested interest in your success and the business' continued success. The seller wants

11: DUE DILIGENCE - (NEVER FUN AND EASY)

you to succeed and do well, because the seller wants to get paid the rest of the money that you owe him or her.

It would also be a good idea to use this due diligence information to do a SWOT analysis on the business and on yourself. Write down what you honestly believe to be the business'

STRENTHS/WEAKNESSES/OPPORTUNITIES/THREATS

and to be your own

STRENGTHS/WEAKNESSES/OPPORTUNITIES/THREATS.

That is a good thing and a good exercise. You will learn a lot about the business opportunity that you have selected through "a process of elimination," and a lot about yourself. And, you will be armed with the information that you need to decide that "all things considered" buying this business (or not buying this business) is the right thing for you and your family.

GOOD FOR YOU! (Next, let's look at closing and taking over management.)

12

CLOSING THE PURCHASE AND TAKING OVER OWNERSHIP

All of the previous information in chapters one through eleven has been leading up to this final chapter, Closing the Purchase and Taking Over Ownership. While they seem two different topics, they are absolutely "joined at the hip." You cannot take over ownership without closing, and when you close, you just took over ownership - so for our purposes, we will treat them as one "VIC" (very important chapter).

And this final chapter is somewhat of a paradox, because like a graduation, or like a commencement, it really is not the end - it is actually the beginning of your life story as the owner of your own family business. You have commenced! Congratulations and welcome to the American Dream of owning your own business.

We have one last "ceremony" that leads to owning your business and that is called the closing of the purchase. This is where the seller and the buyer come together to sell and/or

12: CLOSING THE PURCHASE AND TAKING OVER OWNERSHIP

buy the business. The buyer pays the price as agreed and the seller transfers ownership of the business assets to the buyer, or a designated corporate entity, subject to the terms and conditions of the purchase agreement.

This meeting is normally held at the office of the closing attorney or escrow agent. And, like most ceremonies, there is a lot of preparation necessary to make sure it runs smoothly and ends happily. So, once again we suggest a written closing checklist of the things that need to be done and who is supposed to do them. (Closing checklist found in the appendix/forms section.)

One of the first decisions to be made is who will draft the closing documents and who will close, or manage, the closing? As stated earlier, in a larger business transaction both the seller and the buyer will normally have his or her own attorney and both attorneys will have roles to play at closing. The seller pays an attorney and the buyer pays an attorney. If there is a third-party lender involved in the transaction, they will also have their attorney (normally this fee is included in the cost of the loan.)

In a small-small-business closing, the closing attorney may serve as an escrow attorney and, as such, cannot represent either the seller or the buyer - the attorney is hired to manage the process and to close the deal. The buyer and the seller could "split" that person's fee. I normally recommend using an experienced escrow attorney or escrow agent to close because it saves money and oftentimes it keeps the transaction from becoming too adversarial. I have worked hard to build and maintain a positive relationship between the seller and buyer; I do not want to destroy that relationship at the closing table.

We also need, and we are depending on, the seller's goodwill after the closing to transfer the assets properly, introduce us to the employees, customers, vendors, etc., and teach us how to run the equipment and the business. And, if we are expecting the seller to also be our banker, let's not let our lawyer "punch him or her in the nose" too much before or at closing. (This is not a hostile takeover of the business and this is not a real estate deal, where the seller hands you the keys to the house and says, "See you." However, you will never see him again.)

Small business sales and acquisition is all about relationships. And the relationship between the seller and the buyer of a small business or a franchise is not over at the closing table like it is in real estate; in fact, the real relationship has just begun. Remember, "Trust, but verify." (Good preparation makes for a no-surprises closing.)

Always select an attorney that has experience in closing business transactions (do not use divorce attorneys). If you are working with a business broker, ask for several suggestions for experienced business attorneys that could help you. When using the services of an escrow attorney or an escrow agency, I would recommend that you get the closing documents a few days before closing and have your attorney review the documents on your behalf. (Do not ever close the deal yourself.) This is too important a transaction for you to not make sure that you are protected.

12: CLOSING THE PURCHASE AND TAKING OVER OWNERSHIP

Normally, you could expect that your attorney fees for closing would be around 1 percent of the selling price of the business. However, it is a good idea to ask about this fee when you engage the attorney. Also, the attorney will coordinate with the other attorney's reference, who is responsible for documents. Most often, the buyer's attorney will lead where both seller and buyer have an attorney.

For our purposes, let's assume that the buyer has engaged an attorney to close the asset sale transaction. The seller may have an attorney that has done work for the company over the years and that attorney will "review the documents" for the seller. Normally, you will need to give the closing attorney from two weeks to a month to get everything together for closing.

Let's start with things that need some lead-time to accomplish. First things first. Is there going to be any third party financing required from a bank, other lender or SBA? If so, will they require a third party certified, independent appraisal on the business and/or property? Will they require a machinery and equipment appraisal? Any SBA-backed loan now is requiring at least a third party certified, independent appraisal. That will take from three weeks to a month after the appraiser gets the information and may cost from $4,000 to $10,000. And getting a loan through the SBA takes at least three months after they get the information. (This time can be concurrent with getting the appraisal done.)

Additionally, the SBA requires at least a 680 credit score, some definition of buyer fit, through industry experience or management background, and about a 125 percent debt coverage ratio, plus your house as additional security.

That is one of the reasons that I like owner financing. We have the buyer, we have the seller, we have the lender...LET'S DANCE! Be that as it may, after identifying and obtaining a commitment on any necessary financing we are ready to set up the closing and begin preparing for the takeover of ownership of the business as follows:

1. Who is the actual owner of the assets? (Is the seller a sole proprietor, partnership, corporation - if a corporation, registered in which state?) The attorney will have to do a search with the secretary of state to verify that the corporate entity is "validly existing," that any and all taxes and fees are paid, and conduct a lien search at both the state level and the local county courthouse/ records office (local parish, if Louisiana; French "Napoleonic Codes"). In the case of a corporation, corporate resolutions have to be prepared and the attorney needs to know who is authorized to and who needs to execute the documents.

   Note: There is no title insurance policy like you have in real estate; another reason that I like some owner financing subject to offset in the event of title problems, undisclosed liens, and/or any material misrepresentations that come to light after the closing and takeover of management. The closing attorney will also prepare

12: CLOSING THE PURCHASE AND TAKING OVER OWNERSHIP

a UCC-1 (Uniform Commercial Code) financing document to file on the public record about any debt on the assets back to the lender. This is similar to a mortgage document in real estate.

2. Lease transfer agreement - approval of the landlord and/or new lease agreement should be executed at closing. (The landlord may require that the present tenant remain as a guarantor of the lease for a while - actually, that is a good idea if the seller is providing any "seller financing." It gives the seller the right to "cure" any lease defaults that protect his position on the security interest in the business.) The lease agreement should be an exhibit to the asset purchase agreement.

3. How is the buyer planning to take title to the assets: personally, partnership, corporation ("C" Corp, "S" Corp, LLC)? This entity has to be formed (name search check) and registered so that it is validly existing at the time of closing. A corporate resolution has to be executed at closing authorizing the acquisition. Normal fees for setting up a corporation are from $250 to $500. A checking account and employee identification number have to be arranged for so that the business entity is "ready to go" at, on, or before closing day.

4. The seller will have to provide a list of FF and E that is to be transferred and bring vehicle titles to the closing.

The equipment should be in good working order at closing (or the seller needs to get it fixed at seller's expense or give some credit to the buyer to get it fixed). And, the equipment list should be an exhibit to the asset purchase agreement.

5. The seller will have to provide any and all in-place contracts, leases, agreements and/or obligations of the business that are being assumed or transferred. These should be attached as an exhibit to the asset purchase agreement.

6. Are there any local and/or state permits or licenses that have to be applied for (liquor, beer and wine, for instance; special transportation; health and/or environmental; etc.)? Is an environmental audit required? Note: If there has been a previous environmental audit: phase 1 (history and ground check, neighbors, etc.); phase 2 (phase 1, plus punch a couple of holes in the ground to verify if there appear to be any problems), phase 3 (phases 1 and 2, plus determine the scope and scale of any problems and express an opinion of cost to repair or replace). I suggest that you use the same folks (engineering firm?) that did the previous audit. They should be able to respond more quickly and, since they have done the previous research, just bring up the report to current times at less cost and time to you and/or the seller.

7. Are there any franchise agreements or first right of approval issues that have to be dealt with? How about training issues or a franchise transfer fee? What are the requirements of the franchisor? Have you received the UFOC and have you been to "Discovery Day" with the franchisor? Are you approved by the franchisor to take over the franchise?

8. The closing documents have to be drafted according to the offer to purchase and contingency agreement between the seller and buyer (asset purchase agreement, bill of sale, notes, security agreements, bulk sales waiver, non-compete agreement, etc.), and the copies need to be provided to the seller, any broker involved, the buyer and the buyer's attorney for comments and/or approval. Any changes, and there are always some changes, have to be agreed to by seller and buyer. (Some copies of these documents are found in the appendix.)

9. The contingencies have to be satisfied between the buyer and seller; beginning with the financial review and approval by the buyer of the last few years' (and the last few months') financials. My advice is to have an accountant go over the financials, including the seller's recast statements, and advise you on earnings and suggest ways to improve the business. Any questions need to be addressed to the seller. (Always keep in mind that the financials have been done to minimize taxes - you

cannot change that, your accountant cannot change that, I cannot change that.) A normal training and transition period for new management is usually one month - (two weeks full time; two weeks on-call) and, as needed after that, perhaps with some compensation for the seller's time. A normal non-compete is for three to five years within the trade area of the business that you are buying. (Example, three years within twenty miles of the business.)

10. A closing date and time must be agreed to. Note: prorations of rent, electric, and gas, telephone, etc. are best done outside of closing. This is also true of any "cash draw" agreements. These can be handled between the seller and the buyer directly, after the closing. DO NOT TURN OFF THE ELECTRICITY; have the electric company read the meter on the closing date or prorate the next bill. I once had a seller, after "tight" negotiations, notify the electric company to cut off his power at a restaurant as of the prospective closing date - they did. While we were at the closing the power was turned off - a little problem! Also, have any transfers and passwords needed for telephone numbers, codes, Internet Websites, and any other intellectual property that transfers available and signed at closing.

11. The buyer must obtain "good funds" for any additional down payment or the remainder of the purchase price.

12: CLOSING THE PURCHASE AND TAKING OVER OWNERSHIP

This would normally be in the form of a cashier's check or bank check, certified funds made out to the closing attorney or to the buyer and it can be endorsed over to the closing attorney at the closing. Sometimes a bank wire transfer of funds to the closing attorney's escrow would work; however, the money has to be in the account to close.

All funds for the purchase should be run through the closing attorney's escrow for record-keeping purposes and the closing attorney cannot disperse from an escrow unless certified funds are going into the escrow account (personal checks will not be accepted). If a broker has an escrow deposit, the broker should bring it to closing as a cashier's check made out to the closing attorney, or the closing attorney can simply acknowledge the amount in the broker's escrow as a credit toward a fee, assuming the amount in escrow is equal to or less than any fee due the broker at closing.

12. Buyer and seller need to make arrangements to take a physical inventory and verify that all of the equipment is in good working order as of the closing. In a small business, I recommend that the seller and buyer "roll up their selves" and do the inventory jointly and check out the equipment, the night before closing. (This is part of the training and transition process and a great time for the seller and buyer to "reconnect" after negotiations.)

We usually take inventory at retail prices - then back out the standard industry markup to arrive at "inventory at cost." In a larger business, I recommend that the seller and buyer "split" the cost of an inventory taker service; however, you want both parties there to discuss any interpretation of sellable inventory.

Note: You have heard of **LIFO** inventory accounting (last in-first out) and **FIFO** inventory accounting (first in-first out). Well, in small business we sometimes have **FISH** inventory accounting (first in-still here) and/or **WIFL** inventory accounting (whatever-I-feel-like).

Either way, we have to get the seller and the buyer to agree that there is the normal amount of inventory in the business, as per the contract agreement (not necessarily what's on the tax return), so that we can close. The inventory sheets, even if they are handwritten, should be initialed and made a part of the closing documents as an exhibit.

Also, should there need to be an adjustment to the purchase price due to an overage or a shortage of inventory, as per the contract, my suggestion is that you adjust the note, not the down payment. That is normally the best and most workable solution. Unless your contract is "X" for the business plus inventory at cost. Most small business deals are put together based on "X" for the business assets, including the "normal" level of inventory in the business. And the down payment is the most critical

12: CLOSING THE PURCHASE AND TAKING OVER OWNERSHIP

issue for the seller and the buyer: SMALL-SMALL BUSINESS IS A DOWN PAYMENT-DRIVEN BUSINESS.

> NOTE AGAIN - Our friend "Murphy" sometimes shows up right before closing. You may find that you are a little "short" of the down payment and working capital that you thought you might have. Here are some suggestions and here is one of the many reasons why you always want to keep a good relationship between you and the seller. You might ask the seller if you could "buy" his deposits from him and pay him back over the first year. The electric deposit could be $3,500, the rent deposit $4,000, the first month's rent $4,000, water bill deposit $1,000.

Well, the seller already has deposits up with each of these and it's his money; however, if he would leave them in place and let you give him a note with interest for the rent, water, and electric deposit, that is $8,500 that you do not have to come up with right now. If you are buying a seasonal business and you are going into the "slow season," perhaps you could delay the monthly payments for four months, or do adjusted payments with some sort of catch-up payments after the season. Perhaps you could lower the agreed to inventory requirement and "buy short" or "just-in-time" to pull the needed cash flow shortfall right out of the business.

Normally, the seller is ready to close and go on that "trip to Tahiti" that he promised Myrtle over the last seventeen years; so if he likes you, YOU are still the solution to his selling the business. We may be able to work out any problems. And he wants you to succeed and if you owe him $$$$, he doubly wants you to be successful, so that you pay him.

Some further suggestions for a successful closing and taking over ownership:

A) Try to have the closing early in the day or at least early afternoon, to allow some "wiggle room" for resolving any last-minute issues, changes, or necessary adjustments, and still close that day.

B) Be sure that everyone that has to sign documents is at the closing.

C) Be sure that the balance of the down payment is secured in a cashier's check or already wired into the closing attorney's escrow.

Note: Keep the cashier's check in plain view of the seller throughout the process - there's his $$$ sitting right before his eyes; we simply have to finish this closing.

12: CLOSING THE PURCHASE AND TAKING OVER OWNERSHIP

D) Today's receipts are yours or the seller's; that can be negotiated; however, payroll and other costs should be allocated accordingly.

E) Set up a time for you and the seller to meet with your new employees. I strongly recommend that a seller not say anything to his employees about selling the business until after the closing. If the seller tells his employees before the sale; he has created uncertainty among the employees, unfortunately with no answers to questions. Do they still have a job? Who will buy the business? Will they like the new owners? Will the new owners like them? Should they be looking for another job? Will the business sell? To who? When? I believe it is far, far better for the employees, the present owners, the business and the new buyers to go and meet with the employees, with the sellers, AFTER the closing.

Here are the very positive answers to those questions: The seller visits the employees with the new owners and says how much he appreciates their help, dedication, loyalty, and friendship; however, he and Myrtle are getting up in age and they have sold the business to "these nice people" and we are going to stay with them to make sure that the transition goes well for everyone. You step up and say how pleased you and Mary Jane are to have the wonderful opportunity of working with such an outstanding TEAM and business that y'all have built. (OK, if you are from New Jersey, you would probably have to say "Youse Guys"; otherwise, try y'all.) And you say, YES, you have a job, I need all of you, I have heard great things about you from the seller; in fact, you are one of the main reasons that I bought the business. Mary Jane and I are looking forward to getting to know each of you and your families and to working with you to grow the value of the business for all of us. While, I have not done this work before, my business experience and background has been _____. What I would like to know is something about you. Could we take a few minutes and you tell me a little about you, what do you do, how long you've been here? About two to five minutes each.

F) Make sure that you and the seller are there the rest of the day to answer any questions or individual concerns, and that you are the first ones there in the morning to begin your training and transition. This is a great opportunity to get to know the business, to get to know the employees, the vendors, the customers, and to begin to fine-tune your business plan for growth of your business.

G) Take advantage of the seller's knowledge, experience, and expertise in the business; build an even stronger

12: CLOSING THE PURCHASE AND TAKING OVER OWNERSHIP

relationship with the seller over this transition period and begin planning to add your leadership to your new business.

H) If there is a way to share some of your plans and goals with your employees and include some bonus or upside for them when you hit those goals; you will also find that each of them can contribute some worthwhile suggestions on how they and "their company" can improve and grow.

Congratulations - And welcome to the American Dream of owning your own business! One of my greatest pleasures in life has been helping folks just like you to buy a business and/or sell a business. If I can be of assistance in any way to help you get to your goal line, I would be pleased to. Just call me for a free initial confidential consultation.

You can download thirty years of experience in my book, *SECRETS OF BUYING THE RIGHT BUSINESS (for you) RIGHT* and the twelve companion DVDs to the twelve chapters of the book for only $19.95. The videos expand on and further explain the rules of small-small business from a "street smarts" perspective. I truly believe that a more educated buyer is always a better, more successful buyer!

I can also work with you as an agent and advisor for a fee of $1,000 per month. I can work with you also as a buyer's agent if you are working with a business broker now, or I can help you find and work with a local business broker for a referral fee from the broker with the broker's (and your) permission. Hopefully, I can help you, the seller and the broker to get everyone to the goal.

Now please understand - I am not qualified to give legal advice; I am not qualified to give accounting advice; I cannot serve you in any real estate capacity or receive any fee for real estate transactions or leases; however, I am pretty good at helping folks, just like you, to find value, negotiate, finance, and buy a business for you and your family.

Please e-mail me at edpendarvis@businessbuyersuniversity.com or call me at 843-789-4112, my office in Charleston, from 9:00 a.m. to 5:00 p.m. (EST), to set up an appointment when we could talk confidentially. I look forward to getting to know you and working with you to get you to your goal!

BEST WISHES and RESPECT,
Ed Pendarvis, CBI (Fellow of IBBA)
Business Broker, STUDENT/TEACHER
Sunbelt Founder, Chairman Emeritus

Appendix

Samples – Not for Use

The appendix contains examples of forms and agreements that have been used by Sunbelt Business Brokerage offices to help consummate the sale of privately owned businesses. These forms are included as examples only and are not intended to be used for your transaction. An attorney should prepare the legal documents used for your transaction.

Forms Included in the Appendix:

- Buyer Questionnaire
- Things a Buyer Should Understand
- Agreement to Purchase
- Addendum to Agreement to Purchase
- Asset Purchase Agreement
- Bill of Sale
- Main Street Business Purchase Process
- Closing Checklist
- Preparation of Closing Documents
- Broker Services Acknowledgement – Closing

APPENDIX

Buyer Questionnaire

Name_____ Agent_____

Phone_____ Date_____ Source_____

Resources:

1. Time available to devote to business?
   { } owner operator { } absentee { } management (part-time)

2. Skills, Abilities, Education

3. Experience – What are you doing now?

Motivating Factor to Buy a Business;

{ } Unemployed { } Always wanted own business { } Investment

{ } Other _____

☐ Businesses not interested in:_____

☐ Interested in (mark all that apply, write in other interests not mentioned):
   - C-Stores   o _____
   - Distribution   o _____
   - Franchise   o _____
   - Information Technology   o _____
   - Manufacturing   o _____
   - Restaurant/Food   o _____
   - Retail   o _____
   - Service (B2B)   o _____
   - Service (B2C)   o _____
   o

☐ Other decision makers:_____

☐ Income Requirements: $_____ per year

☐ Time frame to purchase:

   __As soon as possible __Within 6 months __6 months – 1 year
   __1 – 2 years __More than 2 years __When the right one comes along

☐ Capital Resources:

Savings $_____   Home Equity $_____

401K/IRA $_____   Other Real Estate $_____

Stocks/Bonds $_____   Other $_____

TOTAL $_____ (amount willing to place as down payment)

☐ Franchise Referral

* Please submit this form to your Office Administrator attached to the original NDA. The Questionnaire will be returned to you after the data has been entered into ACT! *

Things a buyer should understand:

Reminder to Agents: Make sure you have a signed confidentiality agreement and NDA!

- Businesses sell for human reasons
- Banks rarely finance business acquisition because of the following:
    - tax returns
    - limited collateral
    - owner is primary asset
- Buyers must focus on top-line sales and cash flow, lifestyle of seller
- Top line sales trend and reasons behind trend
    - Down trending not necessarily bad
- Cash flow
    - Business valued and sold on multiples of cash flow
    - EBITDA + owner's economic benefit = cash flow
- Business Value
    - 1.5 to 4.0 x cash flow > most sell for 2 – 3 x cash flow
    - Businesses in manufacturing, with proprietary information and/or intellectual property may demand double-digit multiples
    - Explanations

APPENDIX

- ❏ Seller Financing – combination of down payment and promissory note
    - o Down Payment = 20 – 40 percent of price
    - o Down Payment often = 1.0 – 1.25 x cash flow
    - o Promissory Note > 3, 5, 7 years at 6 – 7 percent interest
    - o Secured by assets of business
- ❏ Highly Negotiated Process

SECRETS *of* BUYING THE RIGHT BUSINESS *(for you)* RIGHT

A ROADMAP TO YOUR FAMILY BUSINESS

SUNBELT.
AGREEMENT TO PURCHASE

1. _____ (the "Buyer") agrees to purchase from _____ (the "Seller") the assets (the "Assets") of the business (excluding cash and accounts receivable) described as follows: the assets include any websites, all equipment, trade fixtures, inventory, supplies, trademarks, trade names, phone numbers and all other tangible and intangible assets used in the business known as _____ (hereafter, "Business") located at: _____

2. The Purchase Price of _____ shall be paid as follows:
   a. _____ Deposit on the date of this Agreement, included in Down Payment to be deposited in the trust account of Broker within 3 business days of the offer acceptance by Seller
   b. _____ Additional Deposit upon acceptance by Seller, included in Down Payment.
   c. _____ Balance of Down Payment due at the Closing in cash with certified check or bank wire.
   _____ Total Down-Payment
   d. _____ Balance to be paid to Seller pursuant to a Secured Promissory note in said amount payable as follows: _____ or more per month (including _____ interest), for _____ months
   e. _____ Additional terms _____
   _____ Total Purchase Price

3. The Closing shall take place on or before 5 ___ P.M. / A.M. / P.M. o ___ at the office of Sunbelt Business Advisors (hereafter, Broker). Closing costs shall be shared equally by Buyer and Seller.
4. The Purchase Price shall include Inventory of $_____ at Seller's cost. If the actual inventory value is more or less, the Purchase Price shall be adjusted accordingly; however in no event shall the purchase of such inventory exceed $_____
5. Seller warrants that at the time physical possession is delivered to Buyer, all equipment will be in working order and that the premises will pass all inspections necessary to conduct such business.
6. Sales tax, if applicable, will be paid for by the Buyer.
7. The Buyer and Seller agree to execute all documents necessary to consummate this transaction.
8. This Agreement contains the entire understanding of the parties and there are no oral agreements, understandings or representations relied upon by the parties. It may be modified only in writing and signed by both the Buyer and Seller.
9. The Seller represents and warrants that it has good and marketable title to the Assets being sold, and will satisfy all taxes, payroll, liabilities and obligations of the business at or prior to Closing. Seller will satisfy all requirements of the Bulk Sales Act or similar laws, if applicable.
10. The following adjustments and pro-rations shall be made at Closing: rent, utilities, _____
11. In case any litigation is instituted to collect any sum due Broker, the Seller agrees to pay the expenses incurred by the Broker in connection with such suit, including attorney's fees.
12. Seller shall indemnify and hold harmless Buyer from all claims, liabilities, or obligations arising out of conduct of the Business prior to Closing
13. Buyer shall indemnify and hold harmless Seller from all claims, liabilities, or obligations arising out of conduct of the Business after Closing.
14. If the Seller fails to accept this Agreement by __, then the Buyer may revoke this Agreement and the Buyer's deposit will be refunded
15. Both Buyer and Seller agree that any information provided by Broker has not been verified by Broker and both parties shall rely solely on their own due diligence and hold Broker harmless from all claims regarding this transaction.
16. Buyer agrees that if it should fail or refuse to complete this transaction within fourteen days after the Closing date (#3, above) unless amended in writing, then any funds on Deposit with the Broker will be forfeited without notice, and, at the Broker's option, shall be split 50% to the Seller, and 50% to the Broker.
17. Severability. The invalidity, illegality, or unenforceability of any obligation or provision under this agreement shall not affect or impair the enforceability or legality of any remaining provision or obligation under this agreement.

BUYER AND SELLER INDIVIDUALLY ACKNOWLEDGE RECEIPT OF A COPY OF THIS AGREEMENT
THIS IS A LEGALLY BINDING DOCUMENT. READ IT CAREFULLY. IF YOU DO NOT UNDERSTAND IT, CONSULT AN ATTORNEY.
BROKER IS NOT AUTHORIZED TO GIVE LEGAL ADVICE.

BUYER hereby agrees to buy on the terms set forth above.   The SELLER agrees to sell on the terms set forth above. Brokers commission as per separate Agreement

Dated: _____   Dated: _____
BUYER SIGNATURE _____   SELLER (Business Name): _____
                                                              SELLER SIGNATURE _____
Address _____   Address _____
City _____ State _____ Zip _____   City _____ State _____ Zip _____
BROKER By _____ It's Agent

Agreement to Purchase_09_04

APPENDIX

SUNBELT®
ADDENDUM TO AGREEMENT TO PURCHASE

The following Addendum and Contingencies are hereby made to the attached **Agreement to Purchase**.
Dated: _____ on the Business known as _____.

Conditions of Closing:

Seller shall deliver to Buyer at, or prior to, closing the following: 1) Consents necessary to assign to Buyer, or assume by Buyer, any property leases the Business is party to. 2) All licenses, permits and franchise agreements necessary to operate or acquire the Business shall be obtained by the Buyer or transferred to the Buyer by the Seller.

A Definitive Purchase Agreement, incorporating the terms of this Agreement to Purchase, shall be agreed to by the Buyer and the Seller. Both parties shall work cooperatively and expeditiously to complete such Definitive Purchase Agreement.

Contingencies:

Buyer to review and approve of all financials of the business
Buyer to review and approve of all equipment of the business
Buyer to review and approve of all contracts with vendors and suppliers, customers

Buyer to obtain financing at terms agreeable to buyer
Seller to provide a satisfactory non compete agreement

The above contingencies shall expire and the Deposit shall become non-refundable without notice to the Buyer at _____ on _____ (Contingency Expiration Date). The Deposit shall be refunded to the Buyer upon Buyer's notification to the Seller in writing, via Broker, prior to said date, that the Buyer is canceling this Agreement. The Business shall remain on the market until the Deposit becomes non-refundable; however, Buyer may notify Seller, in writing, via Broker, that the Deposit is non-refundable prior to the Contingency Expiration Date. In such event, the Business shall be removed from the market until Contingency Expiration Date, after which the Business may again be marketed. In the event that, prior to the Deposit becoming non-refundable, the Seller receives and wishes to accept an Agreement to Purchase from another buyer, Seller shall notify Buyer in writing, via Broker, of said other bona fide Agreement(s) To Purchase. From the date of said notification, Buyer shall have the earlier of 3 business days or the Contingency Expiration Date above, to notify Seller in writing, via Broker, that the Deposit is non-refundable or this Agreement to Purchase shall become null and void and Deposit shall be fully refunded to Buyer. All other terms and conditions of the Agreement to Purchase are to remain the same.

If the Seller fails to accept this Amendment by _____ P.M. _____ then the Addendum and the attached Agreement to Purchase may be

APPENDIX

revoked by the Buyer and Deposit will be returned to the Buyer. Receipt of copy of this Agreement is acknowledged.

Date:_____   Date:_____
_____   _____
BuyerSeller   BuyerSeller
_____   _____
BuyerSeller   BuyerSeller

ASSET PURCHASE AGREEMENT

STATE OF SOUTH CAROLINA

COUNTY OF CHARLESTON

Whereas, BUYER, (hereinafter referred to as "BUYER"), desires to buy and SELLER, (hereinafter referred to as "SELLER"), desires to sell all of the furniture, equipment, fixtures, goodwill, inventory and all other assets used in the operation of the business known as (BUSINESS, ADDRESS) (the "Business"), excepting cash and accounts receivable, for a total agreed upon consideration of (PRICE $000.00) Dollars as more fully set forth below;

Now, therefore,

1. (SELLER) agrees to sell, grant, bargain and convey unto the (BUYER) at closing all of the furniture, equipment, fixtures, goodwill, inventory, and all other assets of the business known as (BUSINESS, ADDRESS) excepting cash and accounts receivable in consideration of the sum of (PRICE $000.00) Dollars, payable by the (BUYER) to the (SELLER) as follows:

    (a) ($000.00) to be paid to (SELLER) at closing for the furniture, fixtures, and equipment; and

    (b) (BUYER) shall execute at closing a secured promissory note in favor of (SELLER) in the principal sum of ($000.00), for the covenant not to compete, as will be set forth more fully in said promissory note and a security agreement securing same.

2. (SELLER) shall deliver to (BUYER) at closing a **Bill of Sale** for said assets in the form set forth in "Exhibit A" attached hereto.

3. The SELLER warrants and represents that the assets to be transferred are debt free, that as of closing there shall be no liens, encumbrances or claims against said assets to be transferred, except as stated herein, and that there are no other parties claiming an interest in said assets, except as specifically set forth herein. SELLER warrants, to the best of SELLER'S knowledge, that there are no past violations of laws or regulations by SELLER which would subject any licenses assumed or obtained by BUYER to revocation or cancellation or prevent BUYER from obtaining or renewing licenses needed to operate the business. SELLER further agrees to indemnify and hold BUYER and BUYER's heirs, successors and assigns harmless against any and all liabilities, claims, actions, suits and judgments existing at the time of closing and not expressly assumed by BUYER in writing, and any costs, expenses and reasonable attorneys fees incident to same, and incurred by BUYER in defense of same. BUYER agrees to provide notice of any such claim to SELLER within ten (10) days of its being made, and allow SELLER the right to defend the claim prior to paying it or making any claim to SELLER regarding it. This indemnification and agreement to hold the BUYER harmless shall apply to, but is not limited to, the following:

APPENDIX

    (a) all liabilities of the SELLER and business known as (BUSINESS, ADDRESS) of any kind or nature, whether accrued, absolute, contingent or otherwise existing at the closing date;

    (b) all liabilities or claims against SELLER or said business arising out of the conduct of the business prior to the closing date, or arising out of any previously existing contract or any contract or commitment entered into or made by said business prior to the closing date, except for those expressly transferred to BUYER;

    (c) any damage or deficiency arising from any misrepresentation, or breach of warranty;

    (d) any tort liability of any kind or nature arising from a tort or legal wrong committed by SELLER or said business or its employees or agents, prior to the date of the closing;

    (e) any violations by SELLER or SELLER'S agents of any laws, statutes, rules, regulations, including those related to toxic or hazardous substances; and

    (f) all actions, suits, proceedings, demands, assessments, judgments, reasonable costs and expenses incident to any of the foregoing.

4. (BUYER) shall be solely responsible for obtaining the necessary licenses to operate the business, which is (TYPE OF BUSINESS).

5. BUYER'S agents have been afforded an opportunity to review and inspect the equipment, books and records of the business prior to closing, and have so inspected same to agents and BUYER'S satisfaction. SELLER warrants, to the best of SELLER'S knowledge, that the books, accounts, records and other documents relating to sales of the business are true and accurate.

6. SELLER, recognizing a personal benefit from this transaction, agrees that he will not, for a period of (NUMBER OF YEARS) years from the date hereof, own, operate, or participate in, directly or indirectly, individually *or collectively, any establishment or business engaged in* (TYPE OF BUSINESS) *within* (NUMBER OF MILES) miles of the present business location in (ADDRESS).

7. Utilities, telephone, insurance, rent, taxes, and employee compensation, as applicable, are to prorated to the date of closing, however, such proration shall take place by and between the parties outside of closing.

8. (SELLER) shall provide a person familiar with the business of (NAME OF BUSINESS, ADDRESS) to be reasonably available for instruction and training to (BUYER) in the operation of the business for a period of fourteen (14) days from this date.

9. The business is presently located upon leased real estate. (BUYER) has obtained a satisfactory lease agreement for the business premises from the landlord.

10. The purchase price set forth in paragraph 1 includes inventory of the business in its normal course, of at least $_____. (SELLER) has neither acquired nor disposed of inventory except in the normal course of business for a period of at least thirty (30) days prior to the date of closing.

11. (SELLER) and (BUYER) shall equally share closing costs.

12. The Offer to Purchase dated _____, 20__, and addenda, where not inconsistent herewith, are incorporated herein.

13. If default be made in the performance of or compliance with any of the obligations herein by either party and legal proceedings become necessary for the enforcement thereof, then in that event, the defaulting party shall be responsible to the non-defaulting party for the reimbursement of all reasonable attorneys fees and costs incurred by such party in such legal proceedings.

14. The business is primarily a service business, and it is not believed that Article 6 of the UCC (Bulk Sales Act) as enacted in South Carolina is applicable, however, if the Bulk Sales Act is applicable, compliance therewith is waived.

WITNESS our Hands and Seals this _____ day of _____, 2000.

WITNESSES: SELLER:

_____   _____

_____

                               BUYER:

_____   _____

APPENDIX

EXHIBIT A
BILL OF SALE

In consideration of the sum of (PRICE AND NO/00 DOLLARS $000.00), and other good and valuable consideration, receipt of which is hereby acknowledged, the undersigned, herein referred to as "Seller," hereby sells and delivers to (BUYER), herein referred to as "Buyer," the furniture, equipment, fixtures, goodwill, inventory, trade names, service marks, related equipment and all other assets of the business known as (NAME OF BUSINESS, ADDRESS), for the purchase prices allocated as follows:

Furniture, fixtures and equipment	$0.00
Inventory	0.00
Covenant Not to Compete	0.00
Goodwill	0.00
Remaining Assets	0.00
Total	$0.00

Seller hereby warrants that Seller is the legal owner of the said assets, and that such property is free from all liens, security interests and encumbrances.

Seller hereby sells and Buyer hereby accepts said Assets in "as is" condition, subject to any other provision of that certain Asset Purchase Agreement dated simultaneously herewith between Seller and Buyer.

IN WITNESS WHEREOF, the undersigned has executed this instrument effective the _____ day of _____.

ATTEST: SELLER:

_____   _____

_____

APPENDIX

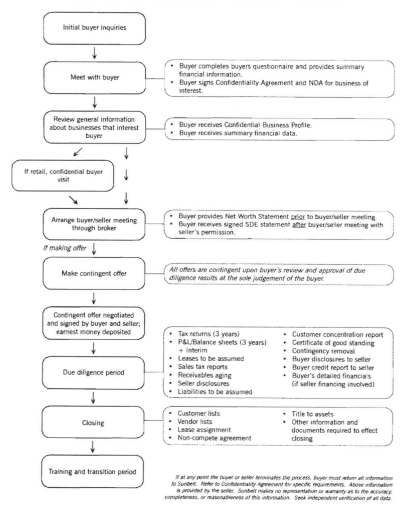

SECRETS *of* BUYING THE RIGHT BUSINESS *(for you)* RIGHT

A ROADMAP TO YOUR FAMILY BUSINESS

Sunbelt Business Advisors
www.sunbeltnetwork.com

BROKER CHECKLIST FOR A SUCCESSFUL BUSINESS CLOSING

BUSINESS NAME: _____ DATE OF OFFER: _____
DATE AND TIME OF CLOSING: _____ LOCATION OF CLOSING: _____
LISTING AGENT: _____ SELLING AGENT: _____
COMMISSION: _____ CLOSING ATTORNEY: _____

SELLER INFORMATION
ENTITY NAME: _____
INDIVIDUAL NAME: _____
ADDRESS: _____
PHONE NUMBER: _____

BUYER INFORMATION
ENTITY NAME: _____
INDIVIDUAL NAME: _____
ADDRESS: _____
PHONE NUMBER: _____

____ 1. Provide a Copy of Completed Offer to Seller and Buyer.

____ 2. Deposit Escrow Funds (Within 3 Business Days) via Policy.

____ 3. Assemble Due Diligence materials (based on contingencies).

____ 4. Meet with Buyer and Seller to review Due Diligence materials.

____ 5. Complete Buyer Contingency Removal Form as Buyer approves and clears each contingency.

____ 6. Contact Landlord to acquire a new Lease, Sublease or current Lease Assignment as the last step in contingency removal; Provide landlord with Buyer's resume and financial statement. Have Buyer sign authorization for credit check.

____ 7. Complete Assignment of Lease and obtain signatures.

____ 8. Complete Buyer Contingency Removal Form for all contingencies. When this has been signed and dated, the escrow money has gone to a non-refundable status. Notify the Buyer in writing.

____ 9. Advise Franchisors of the change in ownership and obtain approval. Enroll Buyer in any necessary training program.

____ 10. Buyer has Formed a Legal Entity. (name)_____

____ 11. Buyer has obtained a Federal ID Number. #

(Note: To apply call the IRS 1-866-816-2065 or www.irs.com).

____ 12. Tax ID Number # _____

____ 13. Work with Seller to form a list of all necessary licenses/permits the Buyer will need to acquire (i.e. liquor license, tobacco license, health/safety permit, lottery license). *Help Buyer apply for these right away…*some of them may require an inspection could hold up the process.

____ 14. Review and approve Equipment List with Buyer and Seller. Facilitate equipment inspection and arrange for repairs if necessary.

____ 15. Contact closing attorney to schedule production of closing documents and the date/time of actual closing. Request draft of documents 1 week prior to close.

____ 16. Provide closing attorney with the following:
- Offer to Purchase
- All Contingencies and Amendments
- Original Lease, New Sublease or Assignment of Lease
- Promissory Note details with Amortization Table
- Buyer and Seller legal entity names and addresses
- List of Assets included in sale
- List of Assets NOT included
- List of Agreements being assumed by the Buyer
- List of Significant Intangible Assets
- Request Corporate Resolution & Use of Name, if applicable
- Request UCC lien searches to be completed 1 week prior to close

____ 17. Create a list all insurance carriers currently in place for the business. Include; Type of Insurance, Name of Agent, Policy Carrier and Policy Number. Buyer must have Binders secured before closing can occur. *This takes at least 2 weeks – don't wait until the last minute!*

____ 18. Buyer has purchased a Worker's Compensation Insurance Binder.

____ 19. Buyer has purchased Liability Insurance.

____ 20. Buyer has established a Business Checking Account.

____ 21. All necessary environmental and/or building inspections are complete.

____ 22. Schedule inventory (usually the night before Closing) and, if necessary, contract a service to perform. Attend inventory with both parties. Convey inventory figures to the Closing Attorney a.s.a.p.

____ 23. Create a schedule of Accounts Receivable which are to be included in the sale as to the complete name, address and phone number of the account and the amount owed as well as aging status. Establish method of collection post closing.

____ 24. Create a schedule of Accounts Payable, if included, as to whom owed, with address and phone numbers, the amount owed and the due date. Establish method of payment at or post closing.

____ 25. Provide Buyer and Seller with a draft of the closing documents no later than 1 week prior to closing. Advise both parties to have these documents reviewed by their attorney/accountant right away to avoid last minute changes.

____ 26. Create a list of names and phone numbers for things that must be transferred (i.e. phone, utilities, address, etc.). Follow up with Buyer to make sure this has been completed.

____ 27. Obtain titles for any vehicle transfers involved in the sale and make them available at closing.

____ 28. Make certain all UCC filings and liens are cleared prior to closing.

____ 29. Provide Settlement Statement (disbursement of cash inflows and outflows) to Buyer and Seller at least 2 days prior to Close. Have this signed off by the Broker of Record ahead of time.

____ 30. Inform Buyer of certified funds necessary for closing.

____ 31. Confirm availability of Trust Funds.

____ 31. Confirm closing date, time and place with each person involved in the Closing.

____ 32. Make sure a Notary Public is available for Closing.

____ 33. Ask Closing Attorney to bring a disk containing closing documents to the closing.

____ 34. Have administrative support available at Closing.

____ 35. Attend closing.

APPENDIX

SUNBELT®

Agreement Regarding Preparation of Closing Documents

Buyer and Seller acknowledge that in view of the important legal and financial aspects and the complexity of the proposed purchase/sale of assets of the business known as _____ (the "Transaction"), they were each advised by Sunbelt Business Advisors, ("Broker"), to obtain the appropriate counsel from legal, accounting and other professionals (the "Advisors") concerning the sale/purchase.

The Buyer and Seller wish to have Broker coordinate with an attorney to close the Transaction. The attorney will draft documents, which are not drafted for the exclusive benefit of either party, which in the attorney's sole opinion, are customary to close the Transaction. Prior to close, both buyer and seller will review and approve the documents with their Advisors. The attorney DOES NOT represent the Buyer, the Seller or Broker in the Transaction. The Buyer and Seller have agreed to split the cost of a closing attorney and to pay the attorney's fees and costs. Such fees and costs shall be due at closing or in the event the closing does not occur, upon receipt of an invoice from the attorney. The attorney will draft the following documents and/or other documents necessary to close the Transaction and attend the closing:

- Definitive Purchase Agreement (if applicable)
- Bill of Sale
- UCC-1 Search
- Promissory Note (if applicable)
- Security Agreement (if applicable)
- UCC-1 Filings (if applicable)
- Consent to the Use of Name
- Corporate Resolution for Seller
- Corporate Resolution for Buyer
- Broker Services Acknowledgement
- Closing Statement

Buyer and Seller acknowledge that the attorney has not conducted and will not conduct any investigation or due diligence regarding the parties or the assets. Buyer and Seller acknowledge that no communication made to the attorney will be subject to the attorney-client privilege. The parties agree that neither the attorney nor Broker will be liable for any representations, warranties, covenants, indemnities or the performance of any obligations of the parties, including any and all claims and damages attributable to the Transaction, and shall indemnify Broker and attorney from all such claims other than claims or damages resulting from the Broker's or attorney's sole negligence or willful misconduct. The parties waive any conflict of interest which the attorney currently has or may have in the future as a result of the attorney's involvement in the Transaction.

Date

_____   _____
Date   Seller

_____   _____
Date   Seller

_____   _____
Date   Buyer

_____   _____
Date   Buyer

Agreement Closing Documents Preparation.doc rev 04.20.04

SUNBELT®

Broker Services Acknowledgement - Closing

Sunbelt Business Broker's ("Broker") acts to introduce a willing Buyer and Seller of a Business ("Brokerage Services"). Broker does not do due diligence on either party. Buyer and Seller hereby acknowledge that in the view of the important legal and financial aspects and the complexity of the proposed purchase/sale of the business known as: _____ they were each advised by Sunbelt Business Brokers, ("Broker"), to obtain the appropriate counsel from legal, accounting and other professionals concerning the sale/purchase.

Buyer and Seller each acknowledge that Broker, nor any of Broker's agents, employees, officers, directors, shareholders, co-brokers, independent contractors and affiliates ("Broker Group"), has not made any representations or warranties, expressed or implied, regarding any fact regarding the business/stock being sold; nor any legal issues, aspect or ramification connected with the proposed purchase/sale, or any representation or warranty to either Buyer or Seller concerning the financial condition, or any matter relating to the other party. In fact, Broker Group has made no independent investigation or verification of any representation, warranty, document, or piece of information presented by either party. Each party has either done their own, independent investigation with respect to such items and was advised by Broker Group to do so.

In consideration for Brokerage Services, Broker Group is hereby released, indemnified and held harmless by Seller and/or Buyer from and against any and all claims and damages of every kind attributable to the performance or non-performance of Seller and/or Buyer under any agreement connected with the sale/purchase of the business/stock described above, except for the intentionally wrongful, or sole negligent acts of same.

The invalidity, illegality, or unenforceability of any obligation or provision under this agreement shall not affect or impair the enforceability or legality of any remaining provision or obligation under this agreement.

Both parties agree that Broker Group has fulfilled Broker Group's Brokerage Services concerning the sale/purchase.

_____   _____
Date   Seller

_____   _____
Date   Seller

_____   _____
Date   Buyer

_____   _____
Date   Buyer

Broker Services Acknowledgement – Closing.doc rev 04.04

About the Author

Ed Pendarvis is the founder and chairman emeritus of Sunbelt Business Brokers Network, LLC, the largest small-business brokerage network in the world with three hundred-plus offices in the United States and thirty foreign countries. He is a 1965 graduate of The Citadel and served two years' active duty in the US Army Artillery. Ed served as director of The American Legion Palmetto Boys State Program for eleven years and as chairman of the South Carolina Department of Youth Service Board (Juvenile Correction and Aftercare) for six years. He received the state's highest civilian award, The Order of the Palmetto, in 1978 by the Honorable James B. Edwards, Governor (R), and received The Order of the Palmetto in 1983 by the Honorable Richard W. Riley, Governor (D). Ed has been a real estate broker since 1970 and started in business brokerage in 1980.

He serves as a member of the Better Business Bureau Board, The Palmetto Boys State Committee, the Board of the International Business Brokers Association (IBBA),

ABOUT THE AUTHOR

and the Advisory Board for The Citadel, School of Business Administration.

Ed was awarded the IBBA's Tom West Award for service in 2006 and was inducted into The Citadel School of Business Hall of Fame in 2007 for his service in small business. He founded Business Buyers University in 2009 to help buyers understand the process of buying a business.

He is a published author, having written the book, <u>Buying a Business to Secure Your Financial Freedom</u>, published by McGraw-Hill in 2005. It is available on www.amazon.com and in bookstores.

SECRETS *of* BUYING THE RIGHT BUSINESS *(for you)* RIGHT

A ROADMAP TO YOUR FAMILY BUSINESS

Buying a BUSINESS to Secure Your Financial Freedom

Finding and Evaluating the Business That's Right for You

Ed Pendarvis

"#1 Business Broker" — *Entrepreneur* magazine

ABOUT THE AUTHOR

Ed is married to the former Elaine Bowen of Charleston, South Carolina, and has five beautiful daughters and seven wonderful grandchildren - "and grandchildren are the best." He is a member of the St. Philip's Episcopal Church in Charleston.